The Death Railway

The Death Railway

The Personal Account of Lieutenant Colonel Kappe on the Thai-Burma Railroad

Lieutenant Colonel Charles Kappe
OBE, PSC, AMICE

FRONTLINE BOOKS

THE DEATH RAILWAY
The Personal Account of Lieutenant Colonel Kappe on the Thai-Burma Railroad

This edition published in 2022 by Frontline Books,
an imprint of Pen & Sword Books Ltd,
47 Church Street, Barnsley, S. Yorkshire, S70 2AS,

Text alterations and additions © Frontline Books

ISBN: 978-1-39901-777-0

Typeset by Mac Style

Printed and bound by CPI Group (UK) Ltd, Croydon, CR0 4YY

Pen & Sword Books Ltd incorporates the imprints of Air World Books, Pen & Sword Archaeology, Atlas, Aviation, Battleground, Discovery, Family History, History, Maritime, Military, Naval, Politics, Social History, Transport, True Crime, Claymore Press, Frontline Books, Praetorian Press, Seaforth Publishing and White Owl.

For a complete list of Pen & Sword titles please contact:

PEN & SWORD BOOKS LTD
47 Church Street, Barnsley, South Yorkshire, S70 2AS, UK.
E-mail: enquiries@pen-and-sword.co.uk
Website: www.pen-and-sword.co.uk

Or

PEN AND SWORD BOOKS,
1950 Lawrence Road, Havertown, PA 19083, USA
E-mail: Uspen-and-sword@casematepublishers.com
Website: www.penandswordbooks.com

PUBLISHER'S NOTE

Both Part I and Part II are reproduced in the form that they were originally written. Aside from correcting obvious spelling mistakes or typographical errors, we have strived to keep the edits and alterations to the absolute minimum.

Contents

PART I

Report on Activities of A.I.F. Component "F" Force

Chapter 1

Introduction

This report is designed to provide an authoritative account of the activities of 3,662 A.I.F. Prisoners of War, who, together with an almost similar number of British prisoners, were sent to Thailand by the Imperial Japanese Army in April 1943. It will be remembered that the Malayan Campaign had terminated on 16th February, 1942 with the capitulation of Singapore. From April of that year various groups of prisoners had been despatched to Burma, Borneo and Japan, but as none of these forces had returned to the prison camp in Singapore at the time of writing of this report a comparison with the treatment meted out to them is impracticable. Suffice it to say that to the best of the belief of the narrators the barbarism to which the force sent to Thailand was subjected has never been equalled in the history of any members of the Australian Imperial Forces.

The purposes to which this report may be put at a later date are not known, and to this extent the compilers are handicapped in that they may fail to place sufficient emphasis on aspects which may become of particular importance in the future. They have endeavoured, however, to record faithfully and accurately all the events, good or bad, which occurred during the eight months the Force was absent from Singapore. Both the compilers were members of the Force and were either in immediate contact with the commanders of the various groups and the I.J.A. [Imperial Japanese Army] Guard, or witnessed the conditions and happenings recorded – Lt-Col. C.H. Kappe, as Commander of the A.I.F. troops throughout the period, was in direct personal contact with the I.J.A. Commanders in practically all the camps and thus had personal experience of all phases of camp administration and control; while Capt. A.H. Curlewis, as a workman, daily accompanied the men to work and gained first-hand knowledge of working conditions on the road. This report is based on the personal experiences and first-hand knowledge of these Officers, reports furnished by Battalion Commanders of 27 Australian Infantry Brigade who acted as commanders of various camps and from detailed log books which were maintained at all camps in which A.I.F. troops were quartered.

The Force comprised 7,000 men and was designated "F" Force to distinguish it from the previous parties to depart. Within eight months of its leaving Singapore approximately one out of every two of these men was dead. Of the balance, practically every man suffered from one or more major illnesses, the full effects of which on their future health cannot now be gauged. Some have been incapacitated for life through the amputation of arms or legs.

It will be established in the following pages that these results were brought about by the ruthlessness, cruelty, lack of administrative ability and/or ignorance of members of the Imperial Japanese Army. And moreover, these things happened in spite of the fact that Japan was a signatory to the Geneva Convention which, inter alia, was designed to ameliorate the conditions of Prisoners of War.

Without in any way desiring to avoid their responsibilities, the compilers, in fairness to the men, feel that it is necessary to say at this stage that no word picture, however vividly painted, could ever portray faithfully the horrors and sufferings actually endured. Incidents occurred repeatedly in which heroism and fortitude were displayed equalling the highest traditions of the A.I.F. in war operations, but the written word again falls short in conveying to the reader what was in the minds of those witnessing the event. These men were not fighting a tangible enemy – they were fighting a far more sinister opponent in the form of starvation and disease. In the former case death was a lingering one; in the latter case death might strike suddenly at any moment from cholera or cerebral malaria, but without cessation it cast its shadow over every man and depreciated his morale. Only too often some of the finest men of the Force and for that matter of the A.I.F., contributed towards their own illness, and in the same cases death, by repeatedly endeavouring to relieve their weakened comrade of intolerable hardships. Camp Commanders were frustrated at every turn. Efforts to improve conditions, such as sanitation, were thwarted time and time again with the result that the never-ending fight for lives was made even more difficult.

Although it was not known at the time of departure from Singapore, the reason for the despatch of the Force was to assist in the construction of the Banpong-Moulmein railway, through the heart of the Thailand jungle, for the most part following the route mapped out by British Engineers some years previously. No accurate estimate of the number of Prisoners of War and Coolies finally employed on the undertaking can be arrived at, but it would not be overstating the mark to put the figure down at 150,000 at least.

It can be claimed, however, that proportionately the death rate amongst A.I.F. troops was lower than that of the British or Dutch Prisoners of War or the vast army of cooly [sic] labour that was drawn from Malaya and Burma. The death amongst the latter could never be estimated but can only be described as appalling. An unconfirmed source has set down the figure at 50,000. Deaths in the A.I.F. amounted to 892, according to information at present available, and an additional 31 have died since their return to Singapore and up to the date of this report, making a total of 923 known deaths.[1] In addition, many deaths unfortunately must be anticipated from amongst the 534 A.I.F. troops who were left behind at the Tanbaya and Kanburi Hospitals and who, with the exception of the staff, were too ill to travel to Singapore.

Deaths among the British component of the Force was more than twice the A.I.F. total. Without the slightest doubt the comparatively lower death rate of A.I.F. personnel was due to a more determined will to live, a higher sense of discipline, a particularly high appreciation of the importance of maintaining good sanitation, and a more natural adaptability to harsh conditions. These matters will emerge more clearly from the report itself and will be referred to again in the conclusion.

At this stage it is not proposed to comment on the work of any particular unit or individual beyond drawing the attention of the reader to the splendid and unselfish services rendered by the medical personnel in the Force. Had it not been for their unstinting devotion to their profession Australia would have suffered a still greater loss of its manhood.

---

1. Since the writing of this report all survivors have been returned to Singapore and the total A.I.F. deaths up to the present date (5th May 1943) number 1,060.

Chapter 2

Organization of the Force

On 8th April, 1943, Headquarters Malaya Command was informed by the Prisoners of War Supervising Office at Changi Gaol that a working party of 7,000 medically fit British and Australian Prisoners was to be organized and ready to move from Singapore by rail commencing on about 16th April 1943. The destination of the Force was not disclosed.

The reason given for the above move was that the food situation in Singapore was deteriorating and troops therefore were being moved to an area where food was plentiful. At that time the rations issued by the I.J.A. were extremely poor and the physical condition of even the fittest troops consequently was well below normal.

The following information was given by the I.J.A.:

1. The climate at the new location was similar to that of Singapore. Camps at present did not exist and would have to be constructed on arrival.
2. The force would be distributed over seven camps each accommodating 1,000 men and administered by an I.J.A. Commander and Staff directly under command of General Arimura, Commanding Prisoners of War in Malaya, who was stationed at Changi. All camps would be in hilly country in pleasant and healthy surroundings.
3. Sufficient Army Medical Corps personnel capable of staffing a 300-bed hospital could be included.
4. As many blankets and mosquito nets as possible were to be taken by individuals, and men deficient in these articles and of items of clothing would be issued with them on arrival at the new camps.
5. A band could accompany each 1,000 men and gramophones would be issued after arrival.

6. Canteens would be established in all camps within three weeks of the completion of concentration.
7. No restrictions would be placed on the amount of personal equipment to be taken. Officers could take their trunks, valises, etc. and Men all the clothing and personal effects that they could manhandle.
8. Tools and cooking gear sufficient to maintain the Force as an independent group were to be taken and specific approval was given to include a field electric lighting set for the lighting of the hospital and Force Headquarters Camp.
9. Transport would be available for the cartage of heavy personal equipment, camp and medical stores and for men unfit to march. The latter concession was granted when it was pointed out that a percentage of such men would have to be included in the Force.
10. There would be no long marches.
11. No boot repair material could be issued at once, but a supply of the necessary materials would be taken forward with the Headquarters of the I.J.A. Commander.

There can be no doubt that the whole project was presented by the I.J.A. authorities in the most favourable light either deliberately or with a failure to ascertain the true position in Thailand, the destination of the Force.

A.I.F. Component

The A.I.F.'s quota was 125 Officers and 3,300 Other Ranks (Combatants) 10 Medical Officers, 1 Dental Officer, 5 Chaplains and 221 Other Ranks of the A.A.M.C. Lt-Col C.H. Kappe – then administering command 27 Aust Inf Bde – was appointed to command the A.I.F. component of the Force and Major R.H. Stevens, 2/12 Fd Amb was appointed Senior A.I.F. Medical Officer.

27 Aust Inf Bde, which had been kept intact since capitulation, was to form the basis of the organization, the quota being made up from other units and services under the command of their own officers. In effect, the A.I.F. component was raised on the lines of an Infantry Brigade Group. This firm organization was the main factor in maintaining morale and discipline of the Australians at a very high level in the months that followed.

Medical Situation

It soon was clear that there were not 7,000 medically fit men available in Changi and this fact was notified to the I.J.A. After discussion, Headquarters, Malaya Command was informed that 30% of the Force could be made up of medically unfit personnel. Lt-Col Harris – the Force Commander – was informed, in contradiction of earlier advices, that the Force was not to be employed as a working party and the inclusion of a high percentage of unfits would mean that many men would have a better chance of recovery from ill-health in new and pleasant surroundings where ample supplies of good food would be available. A large number of British troops unfit for marching or for work were included in the British component on this understanding.

When it became known that the I.J.A. would not accede to a reduction in numbers and that there was every probability that the A.I.F's quota would have to be made up from other than those classified as "fit", Lt-Col Galleghan, Commanding A.I.F., specified that only "near fits" should be selected. Lt-Col Kappe pointed out that the original I.J.A. demand was for 7,000 fit men for a working party and submitted that it was not in the interests of the Force as a whole or of the men as individuals if other than reasonably fit men were taken. He submitted that Malaya Command should make further efforts to have the strength of the Force reduced.

This protest was accepted and this Officer was relieved of the responsibility for the inclusion of men of low medical classification by the inclusion in his warrant of command of the following: "Personnel of "F" Force have been medically examined and such classes have been included as have been required by Malaya Command in accordance with instructions from the I.J.A. The Commander, "F" Force is not therefore responsible for the inclusion of any unfit personnel in that Force".

A medical re-classification of A.I.F. personnel was immediately commenced by the A.D.M.S. and the D.A.D.M.S. from the results of which it was ascertained that of the 2,200 Other Ranks required from 27 Aust Inf Bde only 1,569 physically fit men, 316 men fit for duties in Changi and 100 men fit for light duties only, could be provided.

The Brigade's quota thereupon was reduced to 2,060, the difference having to be made up from other units. Definite figures as to the results of the medical examination of other units are not available but it can be safely said that the A.I.F. component contained at least 125 men who were unfit for work and fit to travel only by train.

In the British component it is safe to say that nearly 1,000 men were either only fit for light duties or only fit to travel by train – many were discharged from hospital to accompany the Force. Their inclusion was to have dire consequences as a result of future events. It is certain also that man for man the Australians were always above the British troops in general physical condition and stamina.

Red Cross

An attempt was made to include a recognised Red Cross representative. On 10th April Mr. W. Campbell Guest – Acting Australian Red Cross Commissioner – and Mr. A.C. Landels, a Red Cross representative, conferred with Capt Machisuka and Mr. Fuzibayashi and made application for Mr. Landels to accompany the Force and for permission to obtain a loan of $20,000 from the International Red Cross delegate at Singapore, on which Mr. Landels could operate. On 13th April Mr. Guest was informed by the I.J.A. to the following effect:

1. A loan could not be granted for Red Cross use with this Force. The reason was not given as it was stated to be in the nature of a military secret.
2. This refusal applied only to this Force and did not mean that applications necessarily would be refused if made with regard to other movements in the future.
3. That perhaps later, when things had settled down and if the Force urgently required money, it might be able to get it then by applying through the I.J.A. Administration, which would be the same as for camps in Changi.

When asked whether they could offer advice as to the despatch of a representative without funds the Japanese officers were non-committal. It was agreed by headquarters that no good purpose would be served by sending a representative without formal recognition or funds.

Final Preparations

All ranks were tested for dysentery and malaria, vaccinated and inoculated against cholera and plague before departure, although the short space of time allowed by the I.J.A. for the preparation of the Force precluded personnel from receiving more than their first cholera and plague inoculations and this became an important factor later when the cholera outbreak occurred.

Every facility was afforded by Headquarters Malaya Command and A.I.F. in adequately staffing and equipping the Force so far as their meagre resources permitted.

Force Headquarters comprised:

Lt-Col S. Harris, O.B.E. in command
Lt-Col Hutchinson, G.S.O.I.
Lt-Col Dillon, A.Q.
Lt-Col Hingston, D.A.D.O.S.
Lt-Col Wilkinson, C.R.E.
Lt-Col Huston, A.D.M.S. – all of 18 Div Headquarters.

The latter was appointed Senior Medical Officer and Major C. Wild was Senior Interpreter.

In the A.I.F. component were included 27 Aust Inf Bde Headquarters, the C.O.s of the three Infantry Battalions – 2/26 Bn Major C.P. Tracey; 2/29 Bn Lt-Col S.A.F. Pond, O.B.E.; 2/30 Bn Major N. Mog. Johnston – and Major J.H. Parry, A.A.S.C. who was appointed to command a composite battalion comprised of other than infantry personnel.

A very strong medical team was selected. This included surgeons, senior physicians, an E.N.T. specialist, an officer with experience in eye diseases, dentists and an anti-malariologist with his special anti-malaria squad.

Three months medical supplies based on normal expenditure were made available from the small reserves held by the British and Australian Hospitals. It was reasonably assumed that these would be sufficient to maintain the Force until the I.J.A. supplies should be forthcoming.

A proportion of Malaya Command's meagre reserve of clothing was made available but so far as the A.I.F. was concerned it was issued too late to permit of distribution to those individuals who were in urgent need of clothing and boot replacements. Unfortunately, this reserve never reached the troops at their destination.

Three days reserve rations were taken and were found to be of extreme value during the train journey and for the first few days subsequently.

As there was every indication that the Force was to be concentrated in fixed camps every opportunity was taken to provide for future entertainment. Both the 18 Div and 27 Aust Inf Bde Concert Parties were included and with the former were four celebrity artists of outstanding merit. Three of the last-mentioned artists and the majority of the first mentioned party did not survive.

It is desired to record here the appreciation of the Force for the assistance given by the Commander A.I.F. (Lt-Col F.G. Galleghan, D.S.O., E.D.) and his staff in fitting out personnel and providing all possible assistance to ensure that the party could function reasonably as an independent group.

Chapter 3

Rail Journey Singapore to Thailand

The Force was organised into 13 trains each carrying approximately 500 or 600 men according to the number of trucks earmarked by the I.J.A. for stores and baggage. The first train left Singapore on the morning of 18th April, and the others on succeeding days, the first six train-loads being composed entirely of A.I.F. personnel.

Trains were made up of steel rice trucks having no means of ventilation other than the sliding doors in the centre. Each truck, measuring approximately 20 feet by 8 feet with an arched roof 8 feet high (maximum) had to accommodate 27 or 28 men. On the majority of trains only one truck was made available for stores with the result that in most cases stores had to be loaded into the already overcrowded personnel trucks. So crowded were the men that only a few could lie down at any one time and practically none could even sit in comfort. No halts were made throughout the journey for sleeping and men were confined to their trucks for very long periods.

With the tropical sun beating down continuously throughout the day onto the steel roofs the temperature inside the trucks often rise to close on 100 degrees, and during daylight halts the conditions became almost unbearable. At the end of four days travelling the men were becoming exhausted. This state was accentuated by the meagre meals of poor quality which were issued at long and irregular intervals. In more than one instance troops were without food for as long as 24 hours and on one occasion 40 hours. The majority of the meals, which were served at any time of the day or night, comprised rice and a thin watery stew containing only a few onions. On rare occasions a small piece of pork might be found.

After crossing the Malaya-Thai border, the I.J.A. Military Police boarded the trains and the concession of being allowed to detrain for the purpose of defecating or for exercise was withheld. No provision for sanitation had been made with the result that the men had either to defaecate through the doorways whilst the train was in motion or risk trouble with unreasonable guards by getting down at halts without their permission, which in many instances was officially requested but refused.

At such places where permission was given latrines were either non-existent or were already completely fouled and insanitary. The condition of these so-called latrines after the passage of the last train was disgraceful.

For the whole five days men were unable to wash except at Padang Besar. Drinking water also was most difficult to obtain and was always strictly limited. On some trains men risked incurring the displeasure of the I.J.A. Guards and in desperation made billies of tea with hot water obtained from the boiler of the engine. One A.I.F. train was without water from mid-day of one day until nightfall on the next.

The Force detrained at Banpong where it was quartered for one night in a staging camp about a mile from the railway station. No transport was made available at the station and troops were ordered to carry as much gear as possible with them to the camp. This short march under heavy loads demonstrated that the men were considerably fatigued by the conditions of the train journey. No. 5 Train (Major Johnston) lost nearly 24 hours in running time and in consequence the party was forced to march on the night of their arrival.

Conditions at Banpong Staging Camp

The day which successive train groups spent in the staging camp at Banpong almost beggars description. Conditions were deplorable and confusion reigned supreme. The I.J.A. Guards seemed to go crazy at their first experience of directly controlling prisoners and became well-nigh hysterical in their efforts to deal with even a simple situation. Everyone gave orders at once and as they were generally of a conflicting nature confusion increased, tempers were lost and many officers and men were struck for no reason other than doing their jobs and carrying out orders to the best of their ability. Special cases of brutality will be cited later.

Each train commander on arrival was handed a copy of an instruction headed "Instructions for Passing Coolies and Prisoners of War" which was to be promulgated to the troops. This, together with the manner in which the Force was being treated, gave a forecast as to what the future held.

It was here that the incoming train parties were informed that they had to face a very long march to the concentration area. No provision was made for the transport of the medically unfit personnel and it was only with the greatest difficulty that seriously ill men could be left. The opinion of the Force medical officers was not considered to be sufficient and before a man could be admitted to the hastily organised hospital his case had to be reviewed by Japanese medical officers or in some cases by Japanese N.C.Os. Invariably the numbers which our medical officers considered were in need of treatment and rest was reduced and many sick men were forced to commence the march.

The camp comprised four attap huts built on low-lying ground in a very constricted area. Each hut had to accommodate 300 men allowing a space of 6 feet x 3 feet for each officer and man. The water supply which was drawn from a filthy well was inadequate and produced only sufficient water for cooking purposes and for one filling of water bottles.

The meals were of poorer quality than those supplied en route from Singapore.

The huts and the adjoining area were in a filthy condition and the stench from insanitary latrines was overpowering. Efforts were made by all train groups to improve matters for succeeding parties but the indifference of the guards and the refusal to issue tools nullified attempts to put the camp into a hygienic condition.

As previously mentioned, no transport was made available for the cartage of heavy personal gear and stores from the railway station to the camp and all this had to be manhandled by men already exhausted from lack of food and sleep. The officers and men's kitbags from the first two trains were taken to the staging camp where they were stacked in the open and covered only by a tarpaulin. The bulk baggage of later trains was stored in a building in the town.

When it was announced that a long march was imminent and all stores had to be carried the men began to jettison surplus items of clothing, those of poorer quality being thrown away and those of better quality sold to the Thais with whom there was a ready market. A considerable amount of trading went on which was hopeless to check; in fact, the Japanese guards themselves took a hand and enriched themselves by acting as middlemen. Although the selling of clothing generally is a matter to be deplored, it is felt that in this case the ends justified the means as thereby men were able to purchase en route items of food which were to sustain them through a particularly arduous period – in any case most of the clothing sold could not have been carried.

So far as officers' gear is concerned, the story is different. Acting on advice received from the I.J.A., Officers had taken with them everything which they possessed including personal effects which could never be replaced. No guards were placed over the stack of trunks and valises at the staging camp with the result that within a few days these were looted, anything of value being sold and other articles being destroyed. Many officers lost all that they possessed including valuable and irreplaceable personal effects. The loss of this gear is the direct responsibility of the I.J.A. and it is recommended that at some later stage officers concerned should be recompensed.

The experiences at Banpong were to be only a sample of the inefficiency, lack of sanitation and cowardly treatment that the Force was to experience in the ensuing six months.

There is no doubt that the treatment here – after five days of exhausting train travel – adversely affected the health of many men to such a degree that they were never able fully to recover.

Chapter 4

March to Nieke Area

As mentioned in the previous section, the Force of 7,000 men had been divided into train loads of approximately 500 or 600, the first six train loads consisting of A.I.F. and the balance British troops. Although conditions varied slightly in the different parties, general conditions were the same both on the train journey and during the subsequent 17 days march. What is being attempted in this section is to set out the conditions prevailing over the 180 miles covered by exhausted troops on foot, mainly along rough bush track through the Thailand jungle. Reference to the section dealing with the train journey from Singapore indicates that every man in the force suffered considerably from the effects of the journey and could not be classified as fit to undertake a heavy march. It must be remembered that it was not merely the case of well-nourished men suffering from the privations and discomforts of five days on the train – quite a number of these men (30% amongst the British) had been classified as "sick" before their departure from Changi, where all men had been subsisting for 14 months on a basic diet of rice.

The staging camps mentioned below were universal for all parties, the timetable varying so slightly as to be immaterial.

After the initial mental shock experienced by each party upon being informed that they would spend "the next few days" marching, spirits rose and morale actually was high when the troops made final adjustments to their gear and set out from Banpong at 2230 hours. The major difficulty experienced at the commencement of the march arose from the necessity to allocate the medical equipment into six or more panniers, and from the efforts made to see that the carrying of this equipment would be equitably spread over each party. A good, flat macadamised road surface and full stomachs from food purchased from the natives at Banpong resulted in the first few hours of the march being covered to the accompaniment of old marching songs.

By 0300 hours, however, spirits had fallen considerably. Practically all equipment had had to be improvised to some extent and rope or wire substituted for the regulation webbing straps; boots, after months without repair at Changi were beginning to chafe and cause blisters; socks already were wearing through; limbs that had to be cramped for days on the train were becoming stiff at the ten-minute halts in each hour of marching; and shoulders unaccustomed to carrying loads were becoming sore.

Dawn found the men really feeling the effects of the sleepless nights on the train, and it was not until 0900 hours, in a blazing sun, that Tamakan (Tarawa) was reached, 17 miles out of Banpong, by the first party. This camp consisted of a padang, shadeless except for one roofed but unwalled cement-floored building about ¼ mile from the River MeKong. A lengthy check parade took place on arrival, cooks and latrine digging parties were detailed, and the men were told the next move would be at 2130 hours that night.

It was at this camp that men first realized that they had to face a future of a hard combative existence, full of doubt, difficulties, defeats, disappointments and dangers. By the starting time the majority of troops, fortified with meals of eggs and fruit which they purchased locally, had regained some of their spirits, but inevitably it was not to last. By midnight the tribulations of the previous night had become accentuated, and by dawn it could be seen that a number of men were in a bad way. That the troubles were not more serious was due to the fact that for the last two or three miles, ox carts and tricycle-rickshaws were hired to carry the medical boxes, gear and many men who had been struggling at the rear of the column.

Kanburi (15 miles from Tamakan) was reached at 0800 hours and a more uninviting sight was hard to imagine. One small open-sided shelter was all that was available as cover for the sick, who by this time had increased considerably. For the remainder, an open space with a few stunted lantana bushes was allotted. Inspection of the ground revealed that it had been used recently by cooly parties which preceded the Force, and as usual no attempt had been made to provide latrine accommodation. The result was that the ground was fouled in all directions, flies abounded, and the stench was particularly offensive. After areas had been allocated and latrines dug, the troops were informed that no march would take place that night.

In view of the fact that the two stages of the journey already covered had been in heavy dust many men took the opportunity of walking another mile to the river to wash their travel-stained and sweaty clothes. Perhaps one of the greatest insults to the men was that the only drinking water available close to the area had to be purchased from the native keeper of a dirty well at five cents per bucket and then boiled. What might be termed a stock-taking then took place. Sick men were classified, surplus gear jettisoned or sold to eager Thai purchasers, medical gear distributed to be carried on the person instead of in panniers, blisters and embryo ulcers were cared for and, as far as possible in the face of a heavy attack of mosquitoes, sleep was taken.

It is worth noting at this point that throughout the journey repeated check parades were called for by the Japanese guards. Almost invariably these checks were ordered at the most inconvenient times. If camp fatigues such as latrine digging, cutting and carrying of firewood, drawing water had just been completed and the men dispersed to their improvised shelters to endeavour to obtain a little rest, a parade would be called and the men kept standing about in a blazing sun while order and counter order was given by the numerous guards all of whom desired to exercise control of the check.

Upon awakening next morning, hopes for a day of rest were dispelled when it was announced that a medical inspection would take place at Kanburi Hospital at 1400 hours. One mile each way was marched to the inspection, a wait of two hours ensued until the arrival of the Japanese doctors, and then a remarkably speedy glass red cholera test, malaria blood test, smallpox vaccination and two inoculations took place. On return to camp a hurried meal was eaten, gear repacked and the men were on the road again at 2100 hours.

The contract set for this stage of the journey was 15 miles to Wampoh. It was on this march more than later ones that officers, medical and other personnel stationed at the rear of the columns had their greatest trials. The number of sick and stragglers was particularly heavy, ox carts and rickshaws no longer were available and the number requiring their gear to be carried for them and physical assistance rendered trebled itself. Some men were so completely exhausted that they had to be carried mile after weary mile on stretchers, there being nowhere at all that they could be left. The pain and additional fatigue endured by those to whom fell the lot of rendering this assistance to their comrades was extreme and undoubtedly the suffering thus caused reduced their own resistance for later days. After this halt every effort was made to keep the sick at the front of the column.

Water points had been arranged by the I.J.A. for this march and at two places during the night water-bottles were refilled with hot water. In spite of these marches being made at night, the humidity was high – within a mile always of the commencement of the journey shirts were sweat-soaked and drenched by intermittent rain and remained so until morning. The dust arising from hundreds of feet tramping along a very dusty track settled on wet clothes and bodies and made conditions still more unbearable.

Wampoh, although nominally a staging camp, consisted of a flat stretch of ground on the river bank close to an old Siamese temple. No buildings whatsoever were available. Two or three large trees provided shade for the sick, but for the rest it meant lying down in a scorching sun and being tormented by myriads of flies. Itinerant food vendors set up their stalls in the area and the men were able to supplement the totally inadequate ration of rice and onion water with food of somewhat doubtful quality at times but nevertheless very acceptable to hungry and weary men.

Some parties succeeded at this camp in hiring a small amount of transport for the heavy gear, the men subscribing one dollar each to pay the price demanded by the Thai ox-cart drivers for the hire of their vehicles. The night's march, commencing at 2000 hours, was a heavy one. The road surface was fast deteriorating and hilly country was being entered. By first light it was again found that many men were seriously distressed. Diarrhoea had weakened many, and as each day passed complete exhaustion among the less robust men became more apparent. At 0830 hours the 15 miles had been completed and the objective, Wonyen, reached.

Once again, all that the camp consisted of was a cleared patch of ground with scattered clumps of bamboo which provided an hour's shade as the sun moved round. Ants and flies during the day made sleep well-nigh impossible, but the troops were informed that there would be no march that night. A small amount of food was purchasable, but prices were rapidly sky-rocketing, quality lessening and the absence of cleanliness in the vendors becoming very marked. The night's rest again gave medical officers and orderlies an opportunity to give more much needed attention to the sick, and when the columns moved at 1930 hours the following day on a dusty hilly road, spirits had revived slightly. It was this night's march, however, which proved conclusively that some men were unfit to go further.

The outskirts of the base camp at Tahso were reached at first light and working parties of men from "D" Force camped in this area were met on their way to work on the railway construction. This camp, the headquarters of "D" Force which had left Changi in March, was one of considerable size and included a bamboo hutted hospital. After lengthy but unnecessary delays, the troops were finally allotted an area, far from clean, and were issued with a few tents as shelter from the sun. Determined efforts were made here for the dropping at the hospital of the seriously sick. Lt-Cols Harris and Dillon and Major Wild, who were temporarily camped there, were approached and these officers made representations to the I.J.A. for this concession. A sick parade was held, and a certain number of men were classified as unfit to continue the march.

The Japanese N.C.O. to whom the report was furnished stated that only a proportion would be allowed to remain. This N.C.O. incidentally had driven sick men in the earlier parties on to the road with a stick. Major Hunt, Senior Medical Officer of the party, paraded the sick men to the I.J.A. medical officer who agreed with the classification. When the party was being checked for the march before leaving the N.C.O. became abusive and attacked Major Hunt and Wild with a heavy stick, the former having a bone broken in his hand. Chaplain Ross Dean was amongst those who were refused permission to remain and at a later staging camp died from physical exhaustion. After much argument only a comparative few of the sick were finally allowed to remain.

The departure from Tahso was timed for 1930 hours. Overhanging trees, pitch darkness, a rough and slushy track following heavy rains, made the march of slightly under 15 miles a heavy one. Unselfish help by exhausted men in helping the sick was very marked. On each night's march from this point onwards it was found that at about half the total distance to be covered a Japanese post existed. Hot water was available and an hour's rest given to enable a survey of the sick to be made and all stragglers brought in. In a few cases instances were reported of men in the rear of the column being struck by Japanese guards, but on the whole no great exception can be taken to the treatment of the stragglers.

It was at this stage of the march that troops were first warned of the danger of Thai bandits attacking men straggling in ones and twos and these warnings were subsequently repeated. In one case a member of a column was attacked but beat off his assailant by a heavy blow with a filled water-bottle. In another, one of the guards with several of the troops charged against the Thais, one Thai being bayoneted and several others being severely struck. Warnings were also issued against tigers. These two threats appeared to have a far greater effect on the guards than on the marching troops and the guards repeatedly showed an inclination to push themselves into the middle of the column rather than be left at the rear with stragglers.

Kenyu was reached at about 0800 hours and in contrast with other camps it provided some shade, being in the centre of heavy bamboo clusters. Washing facilities here were bad and consisted only of a small stream in which a number of Japanese guards took exception to prisoners washing while they were in the vicinity.

From this stage onwards troops began to suffer seriously from the shortage of rations. Previously the extremely poor supply had been augmented by purchases from wayside vendors, but having now entered continuous jungle, kampongs were not seen and facilities for the purchase of food no longer existed. By this time a further difficulty had arisen through the number of men who were now barefooted. In addition, many who were still in possession of boots found that their blistered feet were so badly infected that the chafing of the leather made the wearing of boots impossible and the rough gravel of the jungle tracks and fallen bamboo made every step a painful operation for those in bare feet.

As previously, departure from this camp was made in broad daylight and the twelve miles to Kinsayo were covered before daybreak. Although each of these resting places bore names, all that could be seen (until Takanun) was a clearing in the jungle with possibly one or two Japanese tents. Exhausted men flung themselves on the ground in the dark, still wearing their saturated clothing, and it was not until the heat of the day brought out ants and insects that they worried about the usual meal of rice and onions.

A further night's sleep was allowed at this camp and the stocktaking this time revealed that the rate of casualties was such that the position soon would be reached when every fit man would be carrying a sick man's gear as well as his own. Enquiries from the Japanese guards as to the total distance still to be covered only showed that the guards themselves apparently were ignorant of the answer. The nights had become grim endurance tests and even the fittest were suffering severely.

The next stage was a 14-mile march to Wopin, and here the troops were herded into what might well be termed a rough stockyard, where primitive latrines had been dug by earlier cooly parties and as a result of being left uncovered had become prolific breeding grounds for flies.

On arrival at the next camp, Brangali (13 miles), conditions changed suddenly for the worse. Nippon guards in charge of the camp took control of the troops immediately on arrival and the written instructions headed "Conditions for Passing Coolies and Prisoners of War" again were read to all troops. Men were regimented from the moment of arrival until departure and any slightest beach of instructions resulted in their being struck with heavy sticks.

In one case an officer, not understanding an order given in Nipponese, was struck with a stick about the face and left standing to "Attention" in the sun. After about fifteen minutes he fell forward in a faint and cut his lip badly – this was a signal for general amusement amongst the guards. After departure this camp became known as the "Hitler Camp".

In spite of the night spent at this camp being designated one of rest, rain, noise from the movement of Japanese re-enforcements through the camp en route to Burma and the regimentation of every action made the halt a trying one. It was there that an application for tools for latrine digging was deferred for hours.

Rain at night was now becoming a regular occurrence and in addition to the severe difficulty of finding the track in the pitch darkness, the steep and slippery nature of the surface was causing injuries to limbs. Men falling from, or through, unfenced and undecked bridges and over embankments was a regular happening, and the journey from Brancali to Takanun was no exception in this regard. It was during this march that still another danger was met with and that was the risk of losing men at the ten-minute halts. The moment the order was given for rest men would cast off their packs and, wet or otherwise, fall on the ground completely exhausted. When the order to move again was given it was impossible to tell in the darkness whether all men had heard the call, and on more than one occasion a party would have to return a mile or so to pick up a missing man. This did not tend to improve relations with the Japanese guards.

The site for the bivouac at Takanun was one of the best visited. A cleared space on a hill, unfouled by previous parties, a clear fast-flowing stream and plenty of shade gave the men uplift. Also, a small issue of tinned vegetables in addition to the rice and onion water improved their outlook.

The move from this camp was made in the late afternoon on a road inched deep in powdered dust, and took the column past an established camp of British soldiers who for some time had been engaged in bridge building. Although a distance of only ten miles, Tamarumpat was not reached until first light. Flies, ants and mosquitoes made sleeping during the day difficult, although the resting place was comparatively well shaded.

On departure at 2000 hours, the troops were informed that the march was a short one of 7 miles, and accustomed by this time to judging distances marched and their limit of endurance, the men were naturally very disgruntled when it turned out that the journey covered nearly 15 miles. The halt was made at Koncoita and this was the first camp that could be properly called a staging camp. Details of this camp are dealt with in the separate section dealing with the cholera outbreak. Suffice it to say that, with the exception of the first two parties to arrive, the expected rest at night was cancelled and the men were again forced on to the road for the next stage of 12 odd miles to Lower Nieke, departing from Koncoita at 1930 hours. After the first two miles, steep ascents and descents were continual. It was also from Koncoita onwards that later trainloads began to pass through the earlier ones which had been assigned to road and railway tasks in the vicinity.

The final stage for the majority of A.I.F. troops was in the march of 7 miles to Lower Songkurai, and the conditions in this camp are set out in Part "D".

The extent of the damage to the men's health on this forced march of approximately 185 miles can never accurately be estimated, as they were faced immediately on arrival at their respective camps with so many fresh hardships and so much disease. It is certain, however, that the lack of food and the privations of the past 17 days coming directly on top of the exacting five days train journey had reduced their resistance to such an extent that they were in no fit condition to be subjected to any further trials. Fortunately, there were no fatal casualties during the course of the actual march itself.

Chapter 5

Initial Distribution of the Force and Conditions during May and June 1943

The balance remaining of Train 1 Party, after about one-half had been left behind en route as cooks at staging camps or had become too ill to march, arrived at Tamarupat on 8th May, rested there on the night 8/9th and were joined by Train 2 Party next morning. Orders were received to organise a force of 700 to move to the next camp at Koncoita where they would be permanently established. The distance was given as about 7 miles and with the thought of a short march and eventual rest the party set off at about 2000 hours. The I.J.A. guard, also under the impression that the march was to be a comparatively short one, set a very fast pace and allowed no halts except after an hour's marching.

At about 2300 hours the party arrived, completely exhausted, at a bivouac site which was thought to be the final destination. It was then ascertained that an error had been made and that a further 8 miles had to be covered. This was completed by 0800 hours in the morning, after the troops had rested from 2400 hours until 0500 hours. No water was available throughout the march.

It was at Koncoita that the Commander, A.I.F. troops contacted the Force Commander, Lt-Col Harris, who was unable to give any information as to the ultimate organisation and location of the train groups as they came forward. He and his staff had travelled forward with the I.J.A. Commander by motor transport, but they had been unable, through lack of prior information, to take any action to ameliorate the conditions that the troops were to encounter.

Lt-Col Harris stated that it was evident the arrival of the troops in the concentration area had been too premature for the local administration – if any such organisation existed at that stage – and that conditions would not be very comfortable for the first three or four weeks. He had been pressing for the establishment of canteens and other amenities as soon as possible and realising that the rations en route had been very poor he also was urging the purchase of oxen in order that the men could at least get a meat ration before work was commenced. It is appropriate to state that the Force Commander continued throughout the ensuing six months to press for better rations and canteen facilities but as will be shown later his efforts met with very little success.

That the arrival of the Force was premature was amply proved when the 700 party under Lt-Col Pond arrived at Koncoita (Lt-Col Kappe accompanied this party with the intention of going forward to Force Headquarters as soon as approval was granted).

No meal was provided until cooks drawn from the ranks of tired men had prepared the usual watery onion stew and rice. No cover was available and men were compelled to lie out in the open in a scorching tropical sun until nearly 1100 hours. After some delay an issue of drinking water was made, but water-bottles were not filled again until nightfall. Shortly after arrival the battalion (from now on this party will be referred to as Pond's Battalion) was informed that cholera had broken out in the camps in that area and that swimming in the river and drinking of unboiled water were forbidden.

It was not until the battalion moved from its exposed bivouac to the camp area proper that it realized how serious the situation really was there. Only a few huts were roofed and these were occupied by Ramil and Burmese coolies. The battalion was first allocated an area covered with vomitus and excreta and after partially clearing this area was ordered to a fresh site which comprised a few unroofed huts. Everywhere there was evidence of the effects of an epidemic, natives were lying about in varying stages of death and it was learned that already there had been many casualties.

Prior to moving from the bivouac area, the battalion had been addressed by Col Asami, the Chief Engineer of the area. He said that the Australians had a reputation for being good soldiers and workers in Singapore and he hoped that they would continue to act as such under his command. In conclusion he made special reference to the necessity for good hygiene and of every man looking after his health. He then introduced Lieut Murayama as the future camp commander. The I.J.A. Administration of the battalion was in charge of a Japanese sergeant who, it was thought, took his orders direct from Lt-Col Banno, Commander Prisoners of War, Thailand. After some delay drinking water was issued, but in such small quantities that the men remained thirsty until nightfall, by which time the battalion commander had been able to make his own arrangements.

On the morning of 11th May Lieut Murayama ordered that a detachment of 100 men move to the next camp, about 4½ miles further north, where they would work on road re-construction.

Orders also were given to the effect that all fit men were to commence work on the road in the vicinity of Koncoita on the following morning. It was pointed out to the Japanese sergeant in charge of administration that all the men were in need of rest and that as many as possible should be employed in the camp establishing proper sanitary conditions by digging latrines and cesspits and clearing the area of excreta. There was need, too, to construct a reasonable cookhouse and water sterilising points.

Protests were of no avail, the Japanese N.C.O. reiterating the order that all but the sick must go out to work, as would all officers. Lt-Cols Kappe and Pond were to go out on successive days. There seemed to be no fixed policy as to the inclusion of officers in working parties. Throughout Murayama demanded that all officers excepting one administrative officer would accompany working parties, while in some camps the Engineers permitted one officer for each 100 men, and yet in another they stated on more than one occasion that no officers were wanted. It is not to be thought that the lives of the officers were to be soft and comfortable. In all A.I.F. camps they were utilised in sanitary squads, on wood cutting and carrying parties, on ration parties and on essential duties within camp hospitals.

During the next five days Pond's battalion was engaged on road building and bridge construction. It was during this period that the succeeding train parties began to pass through to the north after stopping at Koncoita for one night's rest.

Most of the parties had to contend with heavy rain in addition to the other trials of the march and were in very poor condition, particularly the British troops.

The accommodation became overtaxed to the extent that the on-going troops were quartered within 100 yards of the huts occupied by the coolies who were lying about exhausted by dysentery or some like disease. Efforts were made to improve the sanitary conditions but with the shortage of tools and labour it was impossible to deal with the fly menace effectively, especially when the main breeding places were outside our control. There can be no doubt that because of the failure of the I.J.A. to force the natives to clean their area of excreta and filth generally the Force as a whole was to suffer unbelievably in the next few weeks.

That the position was precarious was evident to Lt-Col Kappe and Major Stevens, the Senior Medical Officer A.I.F. The former, therefore, asked through the administrative sergeant for an interview with Lieut Murayama so that the position could be placed before him. No answer was received to this application or to many other requests of a similar nature which were made later.

Failing to obtain any satisfaction from the Engineer Officer, the two A.I.F. officers called on the local I.J.A. Medical officer (Lieut Onoguchi) and made requests based on medical grounds for more tents to protect the men from the weather and for the isolation of dysentery patients, for medical stores and additional food for the working men and for a supply of rice polishings to combat beri beri which had begun to make itself manifest. Lieut Onoguchi stated that he had no supplies but would do what he could to obtain extra tents. The information that the local authorities had made no provision for medical supplies came as a great shock. Apparently, the prisoners were to be permitted to die in a similar manner to the natives in this camp.

The general situation was reported to Lt-Col Dillon and Major Wild of Forces Headquarters when they arrived. They promised to ventilate the whole position to Col Banno when they reached Headquarters Camp at Lower Nieke.

On 14th May a written request, this time, was made to Murayama for consideration of the matters of accommodation, food including rice polishings, boots, medical supplies, rest days for the workers and canteen supplies. This request met with the same fate as the verbal ones referred to earlier.

Both the Force Commander and the Commander A.I.F. troops continued to press these matters right up to the time the railway tasks were completed in October. It was only in this month that five bags of rice polishings were issued. The food remained bad, canteens were never established, medical supplies were received in meagre quantities only and except for minor issues of boots and clothing the bulk of the Force remained bootless and, in some cases, almost naked.

On 15th May, it was announced that cholera had broken out amongst the coolies and that next day the battalion would have to move on and join the detachment at Lower Taimonta.

On 16th May the battalion went out to work as usual but instead of returning to Koncoita pushed on to the new camp, which was newly-constructed although it had previously been occupied. As at Koncoita the huts were unroofed and still insufficient tentage was available to cover more than two-thirds of the battalion.

It is thought that the initial distribution of troops as decided upon by the I.J.A. was to be spread over four camps, comprising Pond's battalion of 700 A.I.F. located at Upper Koncoita and subsequently moving northwards on road improvement works; a main British Camp of 2,000; a main A.I.F. Camp of 2,500 and a mixed Headquarters and Hospital Camp of 1,300. This arrangement was varied to meet the situation which the Force was compelled to face.

The Cholera Outbreak

It will be recalled that it was on 15th May that the I.J.A. medical authorities diagnosed as cholera the disease which was causing a high mortality amongst the coolies at Koncoita. Because of this Pond's battalion was hurriedly moved forward to Upper Koncoita.

On the night 14/15th May 1,000 A.I.F. from Trains 3 and 4 under Major Tracey marched out from Lower Nieke to their permanent camp at Lower Songkurai, a distance of 7½ miles. This party was to be joined by a further 800 A.I.F. in two days' time. It was whilst the latter group was being organised that one of the sick was diagnosed by Capt Taylor, A.A.M.C. as a cholera case. The Force Commander reported that at once to Col Banno and recommended to him that all movement of the Force be stopped in order that those troops which had not yet come into the cholera zone, i.e. Koncoita – Lower Nieke, be saved from infection.

This request was refused, and the party referred to above moved out from Lower Nieke on the night 16/17 May. Prior to doing so volunteers were forthcoming to staff the improvised isolation hospital which had been established in a portion of an unroofed hut. By the evening of 16th May three more cholera cases had been diagnosed and it was certain that many other members of the Force must have become infected.

Due to Japanese refusal to permit of any re-allotment of key personnel and the transfer of officers from one train group to another, only one medical officer was available at Lower Nieke. An urgent message was sent to the Senior Medical Officer A.I.F. who decided to go forward himself and take with him Major Hunt from Koncoita and Capt Hendry from Upper Koncoita. Due to the bogging of the ambulance in which they were travelling the two senior officers had to march most of the journey through the mud and arrived at Lower Nieke at about midnight on 16th May. There they were greeted with a rumour that cholera had broken out at Lower Songkurai and the only medical officer there (Capt R.L. Cahill) was seriously ill. It was decided that Major Hunt and Capt Taylor should move on to Lower Songkurai that night. The medical officers, accompanied by 7 A.A.M.C. personnel and 8 British volunteers, all of whom had been doubly-inoculated against cholera arrived at 0230 hours on 18th May. Cholera had actually broken out, two cases having been diagnosed, but Capt Cahill, although exhausted, fortunately otherwise was well.

To appreciate the difficulties which medical officers and senior combatant officers had to face during the ensuing two months the following factors must be borne in mind:

1. Officers and Men were almost exhausted after an arduous train journey, a brutal march for men who had undergone fourteen months imprisonment on poor rations and the lack of any sustaining food provided at any of the deplorably filthy staging camps.
2. Many men had become desperately ill on the march with severe attacks of diarrhoea and dysentery. Men not so affected themselves had lowered their resistance to disease by the physical efforts they made in assisting their sick comrades along and carrying their gear.
3. As soon as parties arrived in their final camps, they were immediately set to work on road and railway construction.
4. The unfinished condition of the camps on arrival.
5. The inhuman attitude of the I.J.A. Commanders.

Lower Songkurai Camp – No. 1

To call this place a camp at the time of arrival of our troops is a misnomer. Accommodation consisted of two lines of bamboo huts running parallel to the road at the foot of a steep hill covered with bamboo and the debris from the construction of the huts obviously several months previously. Except for 8 tents to cover the officers' quarters, no protection overhead had been provided. The exposure of the unroofed huts to tropical weather had put them in such a condition that in most cases they were almost in need of demolition and reconstruction.

Latrines had been dug on the hillside above the huts and consisted of only two banks of wide shallow trenches, obviously a menace to health. Kitchen accommodation did not exist and the water supply was so meagre that ablution was impossible.

No hospital accommodation had been provided for. The huts comprised of 18 or 20 bays each measuring 10 feet x 12 feet in which 10 men had to sleep. It was obvious that it would be impossible to accommodate the 2,500 A.I.F. destined for this camp and representations to this effect were made to the I.J.A. Supervising Officer, who apparently passed on the submission to Col. Banno. This officer agreed to send on only the balance required to make 2,000 and re-allotted the remaining 400 A.I.F. in the forward area to No. 3 Camp about 6 miles further north. This was almost the sole occasion when this particular Supervising officer took heed of any of our requests or recommendations.

The first group of 1,000 had arrived on the morning of 15th May and on 16th May all fit men were sent to work. The following day the second group under Major Johnston marched in. After a survey of the camp, Major Johnston pressed for the immediate supply of attap for roofing of the huts in view of the approaching monsoonal season, and stressed the necessity of keeping sufficient men in camp to construct new latrines, kitchens, water sterilising points etc., and for the re-inforcing of the huts. The floors of two already had collapsed under the weight of sleeping men and some showed signs of complete collapse within a week or two.

It was requested that, as a matter of immediate necessity, every effort should be made to bring forward more medical officers and sufficient serum to complete the inoculation of all troops against cholera, many having been only partly inoculated before leaving Changi. Lieut Fukuda displayed some energy in endeavouring to meet these requests, as he was to do when another cholera epidemic broke out in one of his camps, but that his greatest incentive was the fear of contracting the disease himself was apparent.

Later, on 19th May, Lieut Fukuda intimated that the 800 men who had arrived with Major Johnston would be medically examined next day and therefore would not be required to augment the working parties drawn from the original 1,000. He linked the arrival of Major Johnston's party with the outbreak of cholera and despite protests, persisted for several days in the view that only this party was affected. This officer was to display the same lack of common-sense during the second outbreak hinted at above and which will be dealt with in due turn.

Early on the morning of 18th May Major Hunt, who with Capt Cahill had arrived during the night, inoculated 1,400 men with ½ c.c. of vaccine from limited stocks he had been able to pick up at Koncoita and Lower Nieke. This vaccine had been brought forward from Changi. Steps were taken to establish an isolation centre and hospital for general cases. The isolation centre which at one particular period was to house 128 patients consisted of tents and marquees erected on bamboo stagings.

The construction of this centre was carried on in incessant rain and it was only as a result of super-human efforts being made that the demand for accommodation was kept within the limits of that available. From the beginning camp works were always hampered by a grave shortage of tools which were held by the Engineer Unit in charge of railway construction but only issued for use in the camp in very limited quantities. The Engineers right through were not in the slightest degree sympathetic to any requests made in connection with camp sanitation and improvement, and in most cases, they obstructed the work.

On 18th May Col Banno arrived in the camp and called a conference at which Lieut Fukuda and Majors Hunt and Johnston were present. In the course of discussion, he intimated that the responsibility for checking the spread of cholera and for the health of the men generally rested with the Camp Commander and the Senior Medical Officer.

Without attempting to avoid the responsibility for the welfare of the men, it was claimed that this was most unfair in view of the condition of the camp on arrival of the Force, but it was pointed out that at the same time the policy for the well-being and health of the men had always been our first care. The questions of the supply of more serum, attap for roofing of huts, boots, medical stores and cooking facilities were again raised and Col Banno promised a few more tents but was completely non-committal on the other matters.

That evening the men were addressed by the Senior Medical Officer on the precautions which would have to be taken to prevent the spread of cholera and other diseases. Many of the men seemed numbed mentally by the strain of the long march and by the dread of cholera and it was a few days before they had recovered sufficiently to exert themselves to meet all the demands made upon them. There is no doubt that the forceful leadership displayed by Majors Johnston and Hunt resulted in Lower Songkurai Camp eventually becoming the most hygienic and possessing the highest morale of any "F" Force camp. The employment of all spare fit officers on works, hygiene etc., was a big factor in producing a standard of morale which was to become a great factor in the fight for life which nearly every member of the A.I.F. was to become involved in during the next few months.

Within the next few days 70 tents and loads of attap were delivered into the camp and shelter from the rain and heat of the day was now made possible. After having spent several miserable nights in the open, this cover was most welcome to the troops.

By the evening of 19th May the inoculation of all ranks was completed. It was pointed out repeatedly, however, that these inoculations were insufficient to give complete immunisation and there can be no doubt that when the epidemic flared up 8 days later many lives were lost through the failure of the I.J.A. to produce adequate supplies of serum. The urgent need for a second inoculation was brought to notice, as were the matters of supply of disinfectant, lime, blankets and mosquito nets which had been promised before the Force left Changi.

During these strenuous and worrying days the Camp Commander and his staff were continually harassed by the instructions received from Lieut Fukuda which can only be described as "panicky" in nature and generally futile. As was customary with this section of the I.J.A. Administration every individual member of the Korean Guard gave instructions which they expected to be obeyed instantly. Men were detailed for some minor duty notwithstanding that they were already carrying out a previous Japanese order or engaged on some vital camp work. The completion of essential works was thus hampered and bad feeling engendered. It never was possible for any Commander under Lieut Fukuda's supervision to receive orders from a central source, he would never permit discussion and refused to listen to complaints of any sort made against the attitude of his men.

An example of the futile attitude adopted by this officer is shown by his idea of isolation of the main parties in the camp. The isolation was to be effected by the erection of a dividing fence but latrine accommodation still had to be shared, despite the fact that both parties had had cholera cases. To make matters worse, the creek in the camp was placed out of bounds for ablution purposes, increasing the difficulty of maintaining a reasonable standard of cleanliness and hygiene, particularly necessary because of the muddy condition of the camp occasioned by the incessant rain.

On 20th May a party of 163 Other Ranks marched in, bringing the camp strength up to 2,000. At this stage, 600 men were being provided for road work daily, but next day a demand was made for 1,300. There were 88 men in hospital, 327 in lines were unfit for any duty and 70 only for light duties. After 260 Officers and Men had been set aside for camp duties, including medical staff, only 1,218 of the required 1,300 could be sent out to work.

This caused the first of many stormy sessions in this camp between the Camp Commander and the Supervising Officer. At first the latter threatened to send out men regardless of physical condition, but with strong protests being made on behalf of the men, only 1,220 were demanded for the next day. Rain was falling continuously, yet men were called upon to work 12 and 13 hours a day in an attempt to improve the road which had become practically impassable. This, together with the lack of cover at night and the loss of sleep occasioned by late meal hours, the necessity of cleaning off mud and drying clothes in front of hut fires, quickly impaired the health of the men, some of whom were collapsing at their work.

Up to 24th May the cholera outbreak seemed to be reasonably under control so far. Only 20 cases, of which 5 were fatal, had been diagnosed. On this day, however, the secondary wave of infection i.e., the infection contracted since arrival at this camp, began to manifest itself. The ground between the latrines and the nearest huts was frequently contaminated with faeces and vomitus of men unable to reach the latrines in time. It seems certain that the incessant rain swept such infected material under the huts and along the drains which passed through them. Contact with boots, with patients direct, flies and the lack of covers for food all played a part in spreading the infection despite desperate efforts to localise it.

The figures for this second wave were:

Date:	24	25	26	27	28	29	30	31	Total
New cases:	10	11	35	19	26	26	26	17	174
Deaths:	-	4	4	10	11	10	4	8	51

This crisis produced an hysterical reaction on the part of the I.J.A. Camp Staff and once again the responsibility for arresting the epidemic and the general increase of dysentery and malaria was placed upon the Senior Medical Officer. It took the crisis to obtain supplies of serum which had been asked for on so many previous occasions.

The lack of tools and the men to use them and the exhaustion of the men on return from outside work had retarded latrine and drainage construction. The failure to complete the works programme speedily prevented the Camp Commander from achieving the standard of hygiene necessary to limit the spread of cholera and dysentery. After many protests Lieut Fukuda acquiesced in permitting 300 fit men to remain in camp for 3 days on necessary works. Conditions now had become appalling and only firm control and the highest discipline could stem the tide.

It was at this stage that Major Bruce Hunt made an impassioned and dramatic appeal to the men which finally dispelled the lethargy that had been so apparent, and imbued the men with a new spirit of determination to fight the crisis out. It was one of many such addresses that Major Hunt gave at this and other camps, all of which had an enormous effect on the morale of the Force. It should be mentioned here that most unfortunately the Senior Medical Officer A.I.F. (Major Stevens) had taken seriously ill at Lower Nieke Camp and therefore was unable to take over medical control.

An extract from Major Johnston's report is quoted here to indicate the manner in which the troops responded to the inspiring leadership and example of the Senior Medical Officer in the camp:

"It can proudly be said that this most terrible crisis in the experience of the 8th Division found the high morale of the men of the A.I.F. a dominant factor. Such crises produce the best and the worst in men, but it is always the best that will be remembered when the cholera epidemic at Lower Songkurai is called to mind. The spirit and self-sacrifice displayed even in the performance of the most menial tasks was beyond praise, but praise alone cannot repay the loss of several lives among the volunteer medical and cholera staff during this period."

On 29th May the third day of the period Lieut Fukuda had promised would be allowed for the completion of hygiene and other camp works, the assurance was broken and a demand made for 750 workmen, on the orders of the Engineers. All protests were unavailing. With the cholera crisis at its height, it was decided to frame a strong protest for submission to Col Banno. A copy of this document, prepared by Major Hunt and signed by that officer and the three-senior combatant officers, will be found as Appendix 1 to this report. The following demands were made:

The medical situation was grave, cholera was raging and dysentery and malaria were on the increase and it was estimated that within a month only 250 men out of 2,000 would be fit for work. 800 men had become invalids or had been required to nurse the sick within a fortnight of arrival in the camp and this number was steadily increasing. Demands were made for the document referred to above to be forwarded to the International Red Cross and that work on the railway should cease indefinitely.

Demands also were made for medical supplies, blankets for the sick, invalid foods, improvements in rations, suppressive atebrin, more water containers, waterproof tents and oil to deal with mosquito breeding areas. The memorandum concluded as follows: "As soon as the health of the camp has been improved, which may not be for several months, the evacuation of the area by the troops and their subsequent treatment in a manner more befitting the honourable Japanese nation whose reputation must suffer gravely if the present conditions continue" is demanded.

The letter was translated and forwarded to I.J.A. Headquarters through the Force Commander who endorsed its contents. The context of the demands were also forwarded by that officer to Lt-Col Kappe, who despite many requests was not permitted to leave Pond's battalion and go forward to the main portion of the Force. He was in the process of framing a protest on very similar lines against the conditions at Upper Koncoita and took the opportunity to endorse Major Hunt's representations and to protest not only as the A.I.F. Commander but as the senior representative of the Commonwealth Government in Thailand – see Appendix 11.

Lt-Col Harris stated later that both protests had a most telling effect on Col Banno who exclaimed upon reading them "My God! My God! What can I do?"

The immediate result was the departure of Col Banno for Burma and on his return on 4th June he issued orders that all work was to cease indefinitely. The rest period lasted only four days.

In the meantime, however, the Camp Commander was to be engaged in more stormy interviews with the Supervising Officer, who harboured suspicions that the figures of the sick were being deliberately faked, but was unwilling to make a direct charge to this effect to Major Johnston. After one such scene Lieut Fukuda approved of the segregation of the sick in the camp into one area and the establishment of a central camp hospital for all men classified as "No Duty". The effect of this was to provide a loop-hole for the abolishment of "Light Duty" men, thereby safeguarding "light sick men" from being sent to work, but this was done only at the expense of throwing additional work on the already overtaxed medical staff. 157 men were admitted to hospital on this basis, bringing the total including staff to 1,000.

It was apparent that a "war" was being waged between the administrative troops and the Engineers. On 1st June 300 men were demanded by the latter but after an emphatic protest had been made by the Senior Medical Officer the order was cancelled. The Engineers retaliated by refusing to supply tools for camp works on that day and by increasing their demand for 700 men on the following day, only 400 men being available. This constant fight between our officers and the administration continued without cessation until the completion of the railway.

By 4th June the Senior Medical Officer reported that the fight against cholera had been won, but now malaria was beginning to make itself felt, 40 to 50 new cases being admitted to hospital. The condition of the men can be gauged from the following figures:

Date	Strength	I.J.A. Works	Camp and Hosp maint	Sick in Hospital	In Lines
23 May	1,996	1,267	255	124	350
29 May	1,980	620	312	292	756
4 June	1,924	319	399	996	210

Deaths to the end of May totalled 56 (1 British) – mainly from cholera. Diseases during May were in the following ratios:

Dysentery	35%
Cholera	9%
Malaria	46%
Tropical Ulcers and Skin	8%
Beri Beri	1%
Miscellaneous	1%

During the next fortnight the position was to deteriorate still further, the sick figures reaching 1,300.

The number of men available for I.J.A. work was further reduced by the necessity to supply daily 50 of the fittest men and officers to carry rations from neighbouring camps. A truck had been put in order to obviate the need of employing men for this purpose but no sooner had the necessary repairs been affected than the truck was transferred elsewhere. Rations were then drawn from No. 2 Camp and occasionally from others, and were normally carried in man-packs of loads of 60 lbs. On one occasion Lieut Fukuda ordered that the rations be transported in ox carts drawn by the men. With the road in a deplorable condition these heavy and awkward carts had to be drawn over a distance of 26 kilometres to and from No. 5 Camp. It is no wonder that when the party returned two hours after midnight it was completely exhausted. Reversion to man-pack was made after this experiment.

The difficulty in obtaining a steady supply of rations and consequent reduction in resistance to disease and the arduousness of the tasks which the Engineers were calling upon the men to perform was to cause a further deterioration in health. The rice ration for fit men was reduced to

500 grammes (21 ozs) and that for the sick men to 200 grammes (8½ ozs). The remainder of the days ration comprised Flour 0.8 ozs, Salt 0.66 ozs, Beans 0.4 ozs, Onions 0.75 ozs, and Meat 2.4 ozs. The calorific value of the rations therefore was ?? calories and ?? calories respectively. Accurate records were kept of the daily issues and are available for analysis.

At the same time, relations with Lieut Fukuda became worse. On 11th June, in a stormy session, he accused the S.M.O. and Capt Howells, who was then in charge of the fit men, of their failure to co-operate, of refusing to obey his orders and insinuated that men were feigning disease. The S.M.O. called upon Fukuda to produce an I.J.A. medical officer to independently examine the men but this request was ignored.

Six days later Fukuda discovered that between 30 and 40 officers had been excluded from the figure of 220 laid down as the maximum number permitted to remain on camp and hospital duties. This produced another angry outburst and an order to the effect that only men on I.J.A. work would be issued with meals in the ensuing 24 hours. This order was obeyed so far as the fit officers were concerned but the sick were fed surreptitiously.

With the meagre scale of rations referred to above it was impossible for the sick to regain their strength. A man after being discharged from hospital was obliged to go to work on the following day on an inadequate ration with the result that many collapsed on the road and had to be re-admitted to hospital. The cruelty of the Engineers only aggravated this high re-admission rate.

Many efforts were made to obtain a greater measure of control of the working parties by our own officers who had been deliberately ignored by the Engineers. After negotiation the Engineers agreed that a two-day trial should be given to this proposal on the construction of a section of the road with heavy corduroy. When the work had been completed, although the Officer-in-Charge Engineers stated that the work was first-class, it seemed that it was found necessary to "save face" and orders were issued that no officers at all would in future be required to accompany working parties. This order was never completely obeyed and two or three officers were sent out daily to watch the interests of the men and to give correct reports of working conditions and incidents.

The cholera epidemic can be said to have terminated on 21st June when all but one patient were considered as convalescent. A total of 210 had fallen victims to the scourge, of whom 101 (47%) had died. Deaths from other diseases had up to this date numbered only 9, a fine tribute to the work of Major Hunt, his medical officers and nursing staff. The admission of all men to hospital who were not fit for heavy work had been an astute move and the death rate in later months no doubt was diminished by this action.

From 21st June working conditions had become worse and can only be described as barbarous. Men were being driven like cattle and were not returning to camp until as late as 2330 hours. The earliest that any party came in during the period 21-30th June was 2015 hours and the average time of return was 2130 hours. Men were soaked through with rain, tired, footsore and dispirited.

After their meal they were often too weary to stand around the fires to dry their wet clothing, which by now was rapidly falling to pieces. Boots which had been in a poor state even before leaving Changi were becoming unserviceable and a great number of men were forced to go to work bootless, resulting in numerous cases of trench foot, ulcers and other skin complaints.

Complaints were made to Lieut Fukuda citing specific instances of maltreatment by the Engineers and against the exceptionally long hours of extremely heavy work. He vaguely promised to approach the O.C. Engineers on this subject but it is extremely doubtful if he ever did so. He was obviously afraid of the status of the Engineers and it became apparent that effective action on his part could not be expected. Attempts to gain direct approach to the O.C. Engineers were made but Fukuda prevented any such action. As a result, the only hope of amelioration of the situation rested on Lt-Col Harris's representations direct to Col Banno.

At this stage working parties were compelled to walk 6½ kilometres to work, involving the carrying of logs 14 feet long and from 6 to 8 inches in diameter over muddy and water-logged ground to corduroy the surface of the road. At first 5 men were allotted to each carry but this was soon reduced to 3. Men weakened by recent illness or suffering from malaria and sore feet were collapsing under the heavy loads but were compelled by the Engineers to carry on, at times being struck with tools and sticks.

On 30th June a memorandum of protest was forwarded to Lt-Col Harris for submission to Col Banno. A copy of this memorandum is contained in Appendix III.

For some time, a rumour had been circulating amongst the guards to the effect that all fit men were to be moved to another working camp. Fearful that the sick, who now numbered 1,307 out of a strength of 1,890 may be left without sufficient fit men to carry rations or to perform essential camp services, a recommendation was made by Major Hunt that all the sick be moved to a hospital at or near a railhead in Burma at the earliest possible moment. That this proposal bore fruit is evidenced later by the decision of the I.J.A. to establish a hospital at Tanbaya, 77 kilometres north-west of Lower Songkurai and to place Major Hunt in charge. Unfortunately, its establishment was delayed and the benefits which accrued from it were very greatly minimised. Details in connection with this hospital will be given later.

The whole medical position during June can be gauged from the following table:

	June 7	June 14	June 21	June 30
I.J.A. work – Engineers	230	272	399	275
Camp duties including ration carrying party	420	237	220	252
Hospital	1268	1390	1275	1362
Strength	1918	1899	1894	1889

Disease	Average for June
Cholera	9%
Dysentery	35%
Malaria	46%
Beri Beri	1%
Ulcers and Skin	4%
Miscellaneous	1%
Deaths since formation of camp	120
Missing	11

The missing are the personnel who made their escape in two parties, the first on 31st May and the second on 3rd June, largely, it is thought because of the fear of death from cholera. It had been laid down by the A.I.F. Commander that no escapes were to be attempted without permission being granted after plans had been carefully investigated. Nothing has been heard of the escapes subsequently except that a general intimation was received from Lieut Fukuda that the men had been caught and shot. The escape of Other Ranks did not seem to concern the Administration to any degree.

Upper Songkurai Camp – No 3

This camp was occupied by a party of 393 A.I.F. personnel under Capt G.L. Allan, A.A.S.C., on the evening of 25th May. It continued as a working camp from that date until the suspension of work in November.

As in the case of Lower Songkurai Camp, the accommodation comprised two long rows of huts placed close together at the foot of three steep hills which formed a rough semi-circle enclosing the camp in rear. The area between the huts and the river which flowed parallel to and about 200 yards from the road at the foot of the other range of hills forming the valley was low-lying and swampy. During the wet season this swamp became a filthy quagmire of green mud, no attempt having been made to drain the area.

The water supply comprised a well, two springs in the hills which later ceased to flow, and a small creek which became a veritable trickle of water an inch or so deep in the dry weather. In wet weather the well became fouled by refuse etc., washed down by the rain waters and by the leakage of contaminated water. The river was too far away for its waters to be drawn for cooking purposes and as a place for ablution it was placed out of bounds by the I.J.A.

Only a portion of the camp had had the huts roofed with attap and the men in this case were fortunate to have one of such huts allotted to them. This hut, however, had been previously occupied by Burmese coolies amongst whom cholera had broken out. Some of the sick were still lying about the hut when our men marched in. Even when the natives were placed in adjoining huts the distance separating them from our troops was not more than ten yards. Some of the dying attempted to crawl to the shelter of the hut which the men had occupied.

Food scraps and refuse were lying everywhere and flies were breeding in thousands. By order of the I.J.A. Engineers, the camp water supply had been drawn from a creek near a compound in which coolies dying of cholera had been segregated.

After only one day's respite, which was spent in organisation and resting, the whole party with the exception of the C.O., a medical sergeant, 11 cooks and 35 sick were sent to work on the road and railway.

The camp was in charge of a soldier of the Korean Guards who was far too junior to influence the Engineers, who were commanded by an officer, approachable only through a Burmese Interpreter. Later a corporal of the I.J.A. was placed in charge and in July he was replaced by an officer. Each of these Japanese was generally friendly and did not press unduly.

At the end of the first week the sick figures had risen to 160 and cholera had broken out. Attempts to obtain a covered hut for an isolation hospital had failed and it was not until after the arrival of Major Hunt on 6th June that approval was forthcoming for the use of a small hut for this purpose on the opposite side of the road from the camp. Immediately upon his arrival on a visit from Lower Songkurai Camp, Major Hunt inoculated all ranks with their second serum injection and addressed the men, whose morale at this stage was quite low. His talk had an immediate effect and spirits began to rise.

By 8th June, when Capt R. Swartz, 2/26 Bn, arrived from Lower Songkurai to take over command of the camp vice Capt Allan – sick – the sick figure had soared to 216 and 7 deaths had occurred. After deducting the numbers required for hospital and camp maintenance, and men on light duties only, no more than 80 men were available to the Engineers for work. Despite the fact that this camp was not harassed to the extent of Lower Songkurai Camp the average daily figure of men fit to work during June and July did not exceed 92.

When Capt Swartz took over, the situation can only be described as very bad. Of the 11 cholera cases diagnosed to that date, 7 had died and hygiene of the camp and the proximity of numbers of coolies dying from the disease were factors which may have resulted in the outbreak reaching uncontrollable proportions.

The new C.O. re-organised the group and established a hospital in one end of the huts, complete isolation for malaria and dysentery cases being impossible on account of the lack of cover. Permanent hygiene arrangements were instituted and the kitchen and messing re-organised, and a definite boundary established between our lines and the natives. Even though water containers were few in number, water points were established where all food containers were sterilized, and boiled water supplied to the men for drinking purposes.

The high incidence of sickness had made the men more hygiene-conscious and it can be said that in all the A.I.F. camps the sterilisation of messing utensils and the drinking only of water which had been previously boiled were so strictly observed that disease from infection from these sources was considerably reduced with a resultant lower death rate than in British camps.

Medical stores and drugs available were practically nil and consisted only of the supplies which the troops had carried from Banpong and which had been considerably depleted by the expenditure necessary en route. After repeated requests, a small quantity of supplies was obtained from the I.J.A. at about the end of July.

By the middle of June, the cholera outbreak had been beaten, no doubt due in part to the inoculations given, but the strict control of hygiene during the period that the serum was taking effect doubtlessly reduced the number of fresh cases. The total number of cholera cases had been 35, of whom 15 died; only three deaths from other causes had occurred up to this time.

The main types of illnesses other than cholera were dysentery and diarrhoea, malaria, skin complaints and debility. Diarrhoea was fairly general and dysentery slowly increased during the period. Over 100 men were suffering from malaria, but after the introduction of suppressive quinine these figures subsided considerably. Skin complaints increased due principally to the lack of boots and the continual work in muddy conditions; as in the case of the camps further south, rain had fallen almost continually since the last days of May.

Working conditions in this camp were fairer than elsewhere; work commenced at 0845 hours and the men returned to camp at approximately 1930 hours. No rest days were granted. The treatment, too, from the Engineers was generally reasonable in comparison. An incident occurred on 9th June when five men were struck with a bayonet and injured, two seriously. After a protest had been made to the Administrative Troops and the matter had been discussed with the Engineering Officer, the N.C.O. concerned was punished. Except for the general conditions to which the men were subjected no other charges of brutality can be reported.

The average daily ration during this period was 18 ozs Rice, 2 ozs Beans, 1 oz. Towgay and a small but irregular quantity of vegetables and about 1½ ozs Fresh Meat. No reduction was made in the case of sick men with the result that debilitation was not so evident here as at Lower Songkurai.

No canteen supplies could be obtained to supplement the rations and the provision of any special food for the sick therefore was impossible. To offset the shortage of vegetables edible lily roots, bamboo shoots and a type of wild spinach were collected. The collection of "greens" was made a daily duty in all A.I.F. camps.

The shortage of cooking utensils was always a difficulty. Apart from supplying six rice boilers and a few buckets, the I.J.A. failed to supplement the three 6-gallon and 3-gallon containers carried to the camp from Banpong by the troops.

After persistent requests, 175 blankets and 23 large mosquito nets, capable of covering about half the men, were supplied.

By the end of June this camp was the best in the group, relations with the I.J.A. were reasonable, working conditions and rations fair and the men generally contented, whilst the health situation was well under control by the medical officer, Capt C.P. Juttner. It should be mentioned here that this camp was without the services of a medical officer for about one week after the troops arrived, despite an assurance given by the I.J.A. Interpreter to Major Hunt as the party passed through Lower Songkurai Camp that they were bound for an occupied camp at which a medical officer was available. In response to an urgent request made to Force Headquarters an English medical officer was sent down from No. 5 Camp, further north, and upon his becoming ill Capt Juttner was sent up from Lower Songkurai.

For the state of affairs at this camp the greatest credit must be given to the C.O. Capt Swartz, whose services were of the highest order.

A detailed analysis of the medical situation at this camp is given hereunder:

	June 11	June 21	June 30
I.J.A. work – Engineers	93	89	100
Hospital patients	212	208	178
Camp and hospital duties	85*	87*	103*
Strength	390	384	381

* Includes 10 Officers engaged on camp work.

Deaths during May and June were 18, of whom 15 were from cholera. Detailed figures up to 11th June are not available.

Lower Nieke and Nieke Camps

It will be recalled that after Koncoita, the next staging camp was at Lower Nieke where the parties to comprise the main British and Australian camps were organized and where Lt-Cols Banno and Harris established their respective headquarters.

Lower Nieke were not used at any time as a working camp, the men there being either those struck down with cholera or too ill to march further without medical treatment. As their health improved these men were moved on to the new Headquarters and Hospital Camp at Nieke, 2½ miles to the north.

The Force Commander and Col Banno transferred their headquarters on 11th June but it was some weeks before Lower Nieke Camp was finally closed.

A.I.F. deaths here numbered 11, six of which were from cholera; whilst there were 60 deaths amongst the British troops who were in the majority.

Nieke Camp varied considerably from beginning to end in its composition, numbers, types of work, control and domestic conditions. Furthermore, the personnel were frequently changing. The maximum number in the camp at any one time was 1,075, of whom approximately 450 were A.I.F. and the remainder British. Of these, a number of A.I.F. left for Songkurai Camp at the beginning of August and others later were sent to the hospital in Burma. Even from the commencement conditions can only be described as crowded and after three months when the Dutch entered the area matters became worse.

The site of the camp was a concentration point of the railway system, branch lines and camouflaged shuntings being prepared in great numbers. Situated in a depression, the site was a bad one from the hygienic point of view and heavy rains made the area a quagmire, but viewed as a whole the camp cannot be said to be one that suffered badly from sickness. This may have been due to the constant changes of personnel, although dysentery, malaria, beri beri and severe diarrhoea all took their toll. Cholera also broke out but its incidence was not high.

Rations, by comparison to other camps, were good, perhaps due to the fact that being a railway centre supplies were plentiful. Sufficient rice, beans, towgay, onions, potatoes and meat and fish in sufficient quantities to flavour, were almost constant issues. Canteen supplies also were plentiful. Only 150 of the 1000 odd men were being sent to work daily.

Types of work varied as the months progressed, the principal form being corduroying of the road and clearing jungle for the railway. Hours were usually daylight to dark, and the striking of men by the I.J.A. personnel rare and only minor.

The good conditions in this camp can be said to be due to the fact that Force Headquarters were established there and provided direct approach to Col Banno, the I.J.A. Commander, and to the untiring leadership of Lt-Col Dillon, the Camp Commander. This Indian Army Officer was most adept in dealing with Australian and British Troops alike whenever they formed part of mixed camps.

In December this camp was used as an assembly area for troops moving back to Kanburi from the north and the only permanent A.I.F. personnel there were some 50 or 60 men employed on storehouse duties for the I.J.A., these men having been left under Lieut Wing (British) as too ill to move to Burma or Songkurai Camp.

One incident worthy of recording was the death of Lieut Donnes, R.A.E. This young officer was originally in Lt-Col Pond's party but was left at Nieke when Lt-Col Kappe's group moved back from Takanun on 18th June. Suffering from dysentery and malaria he became extremely depressed and was unfit to undertake the march. Shortly afterwards, while a patient in the Nieke Hospital, he wandered away from the camp at night while delirious and was not seen again. The I.J.A. reported that his body was seen in the river some miles away several days later. It would appear that the conditions of life had so preyed upon his mind that his endurance gave out.

There were several instances of men becoming mentally unbalanced due to the effect of cerebral malaria and to the sordid and at times almost hopeless circumstances. At least two men attempted to commit suicide and it is more than surprising that many more did not succumb to the effects of mental torture. There is no doubt, however, that many highly-strung individuals are still suffering from mental and nervous disorders in addition to their physical disabilities.

Pond's Battalion – May and June

The two matters which created the greatest trials of Lt-Col Pond's Party were, firstly, the number of times the camp was moved and, secondly, the control under which the camp was placed, viz., that of Lieut Murayama. As to the first matter, some twelve different camps were occupied between May and November. As to the second, this officer was ruthless, cruel and dishonest in the issue of rations to the men. What experience in engineering work he had is not known, but he was placed in control to direct and supervise 700 Prisoners of War on railway construction. It is understood that in peace time he was chief physical training instructor to the Tokyo Police and director of the Anti-Communist Squad. 38 years of age, 5' 10" in height and of extremely fine physique, he kept himself in perfect condition. More details of his actions are given elsewhere in this report.

The object of this section is to set out the conditions prevailing in Pond's battalion during the months of May and June.

Briefly the position on 17th May was as follows. The monsoon had broken and rain was practically continuous. Tentage provided was sufficient only for two-thirds of the party of 700, the balance having to sleep on muddy ground under the huts or in shelters made of bamboo, leaves and ground-sheets. Efforts had been made to isolate the sick who at this stage were in the following categories:

Dysentery and diarrhoea 107; Malaria 10; Ulcers 25; Beri Beri 15; Miscellaneous 12.

The ration scale per man per day was Rice 22ozs, Onions 0.66ozs, Whitebait 0.06ozs, and salt 0.16ozs.

During the next ten days dysentery and diarrhoea went up to 177 but had returned to 106 by the end of the month. Malaria showed an alarming rise to 163, Beri Beri a slight increase to 25 but the most disturbing factor was the appearance of the first cholera cases and the first deaths from this cause. All road work ceased immediately this outbreak occurred. The camp was quarantined and the Nippon personnel showed distinct signs of panic.

In addition to these troubles the ration position became more serious than ever – rice dropped to 7.5oz per man per day. This meant two meals only per day of plain rice, the supply of onions having been exhausted. Apparently Lieut Murayama considered that as no work was being performed the issue of minimum rations to prevent starvation was justified. Actually, had some foresight been displayed and a reasonable ration provided during this period more men would have become available by the time work was resumed.

The future looked hopeless at this stage. Repeated requests and demands to the I.J.A. only brought a refusal by Murayama to interview anyone making requests. Lieut Onuguchi, the I.J.A. medical officer, showed a certain amount of sympathy but was powerless to remedy the position. Perpetual rain had reduced the camp to a quagmire and latrines could not be prevented from flooding. Morale dropped to its lowest ebb.

In the light of the months to follow the work and hours at this stage were very heavy, but the dread of that unseen enemy, disease, could not but have the effect of reducing the morale of debilitated men doing labourer's work on a diet of rice and onion water.

It is important to appreciate at this juncture the real meaning of an attack of dysentery or diarrhoea. Latrines at this camp were situated approximately 75 yards from the huts. Some were of the shallow open trench type and some of the 9-feet covered type. At night rain usually was continual. When nature called it involved a hurried disentanglement in pitch darkness from other bodies lying in close proximity in the hut and then a nerve-racking journey across uneven, slimy, slippery ground for 75 yards, feeling for the edges of the latrines with one's feet, squatting on one's haunches for 6-10 minutes with rain beating down relentlessly and then returning soaked through to lie down in a damp blanket under a dripping tent and endeavour to get off to sleep again.

When this process had been repeated perhaps six or seven times in a night the effect was, to say the least, weakening. Furthermore, there was the uncertainty as to whether nature would await one's arrival at the latrine; frequently it would not and fouling of the ground in the vicinity resulted, added to which one had the fear always of maggots or excreta adhering to boots would be carried back into the tent with consequent risk of spreading infection.

The first ten days of June showed no improvement. Malaria soared to 250 causing a heavy drain on the number of men available for work and resulting in a shortage of quinine. Capt Mills and his staff of medical orderlies many of whom were untrained and drawn from the different units, worked tirelessly in soaking rain. Lt-Col Pond returned from a journey to Lower Nieke but could hold out no hope of better conditions although every form of protest and entreaty had been made to the higher authorities there.

On 2nd June Lieut Lillie and a party of 20 who had been left at Koncoita were brought into camp after suffering cruel privations. Left in the scrub, they had been moved into a small cookhouse, one of their number suffering from cholera. All the party were suffering from some form of illness, medical supplies were nil and rice the only food ration. Assistant Surgeon Wolfe, Indian Medical Service, was sent by Force Headquarters to assist this party. This Warrant Officer performed excellent service in bringing the party out of Koncoita and later in helping to fight the cholera epidemic in Pond's battalion and at Nieke.

A typical instance of Japanese maladministration had occurred when after a medical Major had approved of the removal of this party by truck to Taimonta this order was countermanded by an N.C.O. However, instead of being moved the party was quartered in an infected area occupied by Tamils, the evacuation of the Koncoita Camp by the Japanese having involved the leaving of all sick coolies to die. Another significant piece of maladministration was that although the Japanese medical officer had ordered four bags of rice to be supplied to the Taimonta Camp a Corporal allowed only three bags to be used while on the same day rice could be purchased from Tamils in the area at the price of $1.00 for 3lbs. Without doubt somebody responsible was aware of this dishonesty which was taking place in the cookhouse.

On 6th June the camp strength was 694, four deaths from cholera having occurred. Of this total 368 were too ill for work even of the lightest nature. On 8th June the ration position was so serious that the I.J.A. decided to send 316 all ranks, including fit and light duty men, to Nieke.

With the object of establishing contact with Col Banno through Force Headquarters which still was at Lower Nieke, Lt-Col Kappe accompanied this party.

Some ox carts had been provided for the cartage of tents, heavy cooking gear and engineer tools but the party had not travelled more than 400 yards before it was found necessary to allot 20 men to assist the oxen. This number was found to be insufficient and at times as many as 50 men could be seen floundering in the mud assisting the beasts to get the carts through. At the end of the day the oxen had been dispensed with and the convoy arrived after a 9-hour struggle at a small camp only 5 kilometres from its starting point.

The night was wet and there was insufficient cover for everyone. Next day about 10 kilometres were covered in the same number of hours, this time the men carrying the tents and camp stores. The night was spent at Lower Nieke (Headquarters Camp) and the opportunity was taken by Lt-Col Kappe to discuss the general position with Lt-Col Harris for the first time. The latter was of the opinion that Pond's battalion would be concentrated with the rest of the Force in the Nieke area and as conditions there were known to be better than at Taimonta a general improvement could be anticipated. In an interview Lt-Col Kappe gained the impression that Col Banno was sincere when he frankly deplored the conditions to which the Force was being subjected and when he stated that he was doing all in his power to meet various requests which the Force Commander had made to him.

Next day, the 10th, the battalion moved on to Nieke Camp but after accommodation had been fixed and arrangements made for a permanent stay, it was informed that its new camp in tents was to be established on the river bank about 1 kilometre south of the main camp and that it would not come under the jurisdiction of Force Headquarters. A large number of Burmese already were encamped at this location. Sanitation was as usual non-existent; excreta, both human and ox dung, lay everywhere and flies were breeding in thousands. It was obvious that too many of the natives were suffering from dysentery and it was possible that some had contracted cholera.

After an area had been allotted an attempt was made to have the coolies removed without success.

On 11th June the jungle was cleared and the tents, many of them not waterproof, were erected. Twelve-man tents had perforce to shelter 30 men and in some cases even more.

After three days of marching through knee-deep mud most of the men were exhausted and in need of rest, yet work parties for the building of bridges and reconstruction of the road to the south were called out on 12th June. Over one hundred men were found to be unfit for work and only 170 could be provided.

The promise of better rations was only partly fulfilled, the daily scale being Rice 13 ozs; Whitebait 1.6 ozs; Beans 1.5 ozs; Onions 0.5 ozs; Salt 0.2 ozs. This matter was referred to Lieut Murayama who had come forward with the party and a comparison made with the Changi ration for working men. A little fresh meat was issued from time to time and this was increased on occasions by illegal methods which later were to be detected.

On 12th June Lt-Col Harris, Lt-Col Banno and about 50 men from Lower Nieke passed through en route to the new headquarters camp at Nieke. The situation regarding tentage, the fact that the party had no medical officer and that there was a grave shortage of quinine for the treatment of malaria was reported to them. Actually 2,000 tablets were received later in the day through the initiative of Sgt Bowan, R.A.P. Sgt 2/29 Bn, who was in charge of the sick.

On the following day the rice ration was reduced to 9 ozs. A protest against this and requests for medical supplies, tents and for arrangements for a medical officer to be attached from Nieke were made to Lieut Murayama but as usual were ignored.

On 14th June the number of 158 sick was queried by Murayama and a medical examination was carried out by a representative of the Japanese Medical Service. The classifications made by Sgt Bowan were agreed with. To save face Murayama then ordered all officers including Lt-Col Kappe to go out to work daily. The officers, many of whom were ill, had been performing useful tasks in camp on sanitation, fuel collecting, etc.

On 17th June trouble arose over some oxen which the men had found straying in the bush and killed. All forms of punishment were threatened if the culprits were not handed over. As everyone in the camp including the Commander had partaken of the meat the whole matter deliberately was misrepresented. There can be no doubt that the health of many men was saved by the extra food which they had received from this illegal source.

Up to this stage it had been impossible to discover who was the authority responsible for camp control. A protest against the conditions at Upper Koncoita and a request for investigation by the International Red Cross had been submitted to Col Banno on 28th May. The only immediate result from this protest was a promise from Col Banno that he would personally visit Pond's battalion, but soon afterwards it was discovered that Lieut Murayama's party was outside the I.J.A. Commander's jurisdiction and the visit was not forthcoming. A summary of the protests is as follows:

1. The food situation was serious. Men had lived on rice and onion water for 18 days during the long and arduous march from Banpong through insanitary staging camps and were so debilitated by conditions that they were hardly fit for work and had little resistance to disease such as cholera, dysentery, etc. The rice ration had been reduced from 4½ bags to 2 bags which was only sufficient for two meals per day. Issues of beans and towgay were negligible.
2. Cover from the weather was inadequate, the men's boots were becoming unserviceable and there was a shortage of clothing.
3. The problem of supply in this area was appreciated but it was pointed out that hundreds of lives were being endangered.
4. A request was made for special food for the sick.

Entry on to the second ten days of June showed that every man was suffering severely from hunger pains, weakness and giddiness although the rice ration had been increased to 12.5 ozs per man per day. Malaria, proportionately to the number of men left in camp remained at the same figure of one in three. Dysentery on the other hand had increased considerably and on the non-malarials one in five were sufferers. Diphtheria had been added to the list of other illnesses and by 20th June of the remaining 233 men only 60 were not classified as sick in some form or other.

On 12th and 16th June two further parties of 70 and 92 respectively were moved to Nieke, practically every man being either a 3-day old malaria case or suffering from diarrhoea. By road the distance to the new camp was 13 miles but rain fell continuously and distances became considerably increased by the necessity to zig-zag on hills and make detours round swamps.

The men pitched sodden tents at night and had to content themselves with 4 ozs plain rice. The third party of 92 were inhumanely burdened with their own gear, wet tents, heavy coils of engineer wire, I.J.A. Red Cross stores and rations cased in heavy boxes, bundles of picks and shovels and even the sentries' packs and rifles were added to the overloaded men. This party – under Capt Curlewis – after a gruelling trip were told immediately on arrival at 1700 hours that the whole party of 386 would return again at 0600 hours the next morning. Of the grand total, 54 of the sickest men were allowed to remain and later were moved forward to Nieke Hospital Base Camp.

On 18th June withdrawal commenced, and from that date until 2nd July the whole of Pond's battalion (the balance of Tainonta being picked up en route) was again on the road under appalling conditions. Hopelessly weighed down with equipment, steps were retraced through mud and slime. From Nieke River to Upper Koncoita, from Upper Koncoita to Koncoita, from Koncoita to Krion Krai, from Krion Krai to Tamarumpat, from Tamarumpat to Takanun, a distance of 39 miles, a shuttle system had to be employed whereby fit and nearly fit (who by now were very few) marched to the next camp, erected tents, dug latrines, prepared cookhouses etc and then returned to the last camp to carry stretcher cases and sick men and their gear forward.

To add the last straw to these trials the men repeatedly were ordered back to dig out from the mud and then push up the hills the many ox carts laden with Japanese stores which had become bogged. Over and over again these efforts kept the men on the road until 3 and 4 o'clock in the morning, only to start again at 0800 hours.

At Koncoita, where the party halted for two days the troops were billeted in huts evacuated the previous day on account of cholera deaths. The huts were indescribably filthy and protests only caused the Force to realise that they were officially placed on the same level as Burmese coolies. An application for tools with which to clean up the filth had brought the reply that none was available despite the fact that hundreds of shovels and chunkels had been brought forward from Upper Koncoita.

Coolies walked through the huts, spat, defaecated and vomited and mixed everywhere; yak carts and yelling drivers congregated at the entrance, yaks were taken through the huts and dropped their excreta where rice bags had to be stored. It was from this camp that Lt-Col Kappe, under pretence to the Nipponese that he had been ordered back to Nieke by Col Banno, undertook to return again to Nieke to voice a protest against the inhumane conditions. The ruse was a deliberate lie to the Japanese sergeant but it succeeded. Upon arrival at Nieke he reported to the Force Commander the shocking conditions which Pond's battalion had had to endure and in a written report to Col Banno he outlined the position as indicated above.

The orders for departure from this camp were as usual issued late at night which involved all arrangements for packing, detailing of carrying parties etc. being made in pitch darkness as the move had to commence at first light. Incidentally the night was made hideous by the screams of pain from coolies as they died from cholera, and yells as others fought amongst themselves for some inconsiderable trifle.

The following figures give an indication of the health position in Pond's battalion during May-June:

At Upper Koncoita	May 24	May 31	June 10	June 20
Cholera	–	4	4	3
Malaria	45	163	210	85
Dysentery & Diarrhoea	170	107	68	50
Ulcers & Skin	37	25	15	10
Beri Beri	16	20	21	12
Miscellaneous	13	8	10	13
Total sick	281	327	326	173
Strength	698	698	385*	233
Percentage of sick	40%	47%	86%	74%

* Strength reduced by move of party to Nieke river.

Chapter 6

Conditions during July

With the advent of July the monsoon set in in real earnest. The road, if such a ribbon of mud can be called such, had become almost impassable, except by a few six-wheeled Japanese lorries which were transporting rations from Burma to Nieke, which place obviously was being developed as an advanced base. In the north bridges were being repeatedly washed away and convoys to Nieke were most irregular.

When vehicles could get through no thought was given to off-loading say 10 bags of rice and a few other stores daily for the personnel in Lower Songkurai Camp who still had to trudge through the rain and mud to Songkurai Camp to draw supplies. Below Nieke road conditions were even worse and in the vicinity of Tainonta the newly laid out road on which Pond's battalion had worked was nothing more than a quagmire through which no transport could move. Troops at Lower Nieke left behind to look after the very sick had also to manhandle rations from Nieke.

More than half the Force was without boots by this time with the result that many men were suffering from trench foot and poisoned sores which quickly developed into tropical ulcers of the most acute type. Bandages and surgical dressings had not been issued in anything but a small quantity and dressings for the hundreds of tropical ulcers had to be improvised from banana leaves, scraps of clothing and any rags which could be found.

The issue of blankets had not been wide enough to permit of giving cover and warmth to even the very sick fever cases. No clothing or boots had yet been issued and the men were almost naked. Men were going to work in the scantiest of loin cloths, pieces of towelling or bits of rag wrapped around their middles.

Lower Songkurai Camp – No. 1

On 1st July Lt-Col Kappe arrived at this camp and took over command from Major Johnston. His plan for establishing a small A.I.F. Headquarters where records could be centralised and from where he could watch the interests of the A.I.F. personnel in the other camps was frustrated by the orders of Lieut. Fukuda who forbade inter-camp movement. Communications with Force Headquarters which had now moved to Nieke was always a precarious matter. Memoranda were handed surreptitiously to truck drivers who on many occasions were not able to effect delivery for weeks. Some communications never reached their intended recipients. There can be no doubt that the I.J.A. were determined to thwart any form of control by either the Force Commander or Commander A.I.F. troops.

Great hopes were entertained from the fact that initial steps had been taken by the administration to establish a hospital in Burma. On 29th June Lieut Tanio (I.J.A. Medical Officer) accompanied by Major R.H. Anderson and Capt. J Taylor, the latter two officers from Lower Songkurai, left to make preliminary arrangements for the establishment of a 2000-bed hospital. The site selected for the hospital was at Tanbaya, the then railhead in Burma 48 miles from Lower Songkurai Camp.

Lieut Tanio indicated that the evacuation of sick would commence almost immediately after their return. This news acted as a great fillip to the spirits of the sick and to Camp Commanders and Medical Officers who now saw a chance of saving many lives. Unfortunately the subsequent bungling causing delay was to result in many men losing their lives before they could be removed from their present hospitals.

Hardly a day during the month of July was free from incident. The loss of a pick on 2nd July resulted in a Fukuda ultimatum to the effect that the whole camp including the sick and workers would not be fed until the pick was found. A spirited protest was made against the stoppage of food for the workers and sick and Fukuda "graciously" commuted the punishment to exclude these men. Next day the pick was found, obviously having been replaced by a man who mislaid it and was afraid to report the matter for fear of drastic punishment by the I.J.A. Fukuda then stated that the camp would continue to starve until the culprit had been produced. After further protests the sick and outside workers again were excluded. It was not until 1600 hours that the matter was finalised and the camp fed.

Working conditions deteriorated. Work did not finish until 2100 hours when the men had to face a two-hour march through the rain and mud in pitch black darkness. On 7th July a protest against the maltreatment of men was forwarded to Force Headquarters. This pointed out that on 3rd July men marched out of camp at 0900 hours and after ploughing through the mud for 5 kilometres commenced work at 1030.

The task for the day for 135 men was 160 metres of corduroying. This involved removal of the mud for a width of 6 feet, laying the logs, draining and re-inforcing the track with earth and stones. Parties of 10-12 men were forced to carry in the day seven logs 15 feet long and 10-12 inches in diameter a distance of one kilometre through the mud and slush. Four men collapsed. In one instance only six men were detailed to a log. They were driven along by an Engineer who struck the men every 10 yards or so with a bamboo stick. Up to 1345 hours the men had been given no rest, then after a break of 30 minutes for lunch they had to work on until 2100 hours with one rest of 15 minutes, returning to camp at 2230 hours.

The working hours next day were the same except that there was not even a break during the afternoon. Instead of 10-12 men being allotted to each log carrying party, there were only seven. Eight men collapsed under the heavy load – one, a Sergeant, fell to the ground completely exhausted but was flogged and forced to carry on.

The escape from Songkurai Camp by several British Officers threw the whole of the P.O.W. Administration into a frenzy. Picquets consisting of Prisoners of War were posted in passageways and outside huts and around the perimeter of the camp, absorbing some 70 Light Duty men daily. For the work of guarding the camp these men were not included in the pay roll. The escape of those officers certainly had a distinct bearing on the attitude of the guards to the Force generally. Previously there had been some freedom of movement in the vicinity of the camp but this now was stopped. Nothing could persuade Col Banno that both Lt-Col Hingston, Commander of Songkurai Camp, and Lt-Col Harris were not accessories to the escape. To the latter Col Banno would not speak for a month.

As a result, all officers' pay and bulk funds held by the A.I.F. Commander had to be handed in to Lieut Fukuda and could only be obtained from him for specific purposes. This was in no way inconvenient since Fukuda had stopped buying parties from going to Nieke village for the purchase of tobacco and other items of canteen supplies. It was not until after many requests had been made that purchases of any nature were permitted and these through the I.J.A. guards who obviously were lining their pockets with commission.

The fight for increased rations went on daily and it was after repeated demands that the rice ration for hospital patients was increased to 14.3 ozs and that approval was obtained to establish a convalescent section within the hospital where men would obtain 21 ozs of rice daily. The ration for men on I.J.A. work remained at 25 ozs and it was now possible to give the heavy workers their full entitlement instead of deducting a portion to feed the sick who up to this stage were almost starving. An issue of 21 to 25 ozs may appear an ample ration on the surface, but it must be remembered that the scale of supplementary rations was almost negligible.

The average daily ration during the month of July in this camp – apart from the rice mentioned above – was Beans 1.76 ozs; Meat 1.2 ozs; Salt 0.5 ozs; Towgay 0.5 ozs; Onions 0.6 ozs; six gallons of oil were issued to the camp of an average strength of over 1,880 for the whole month. With the inability to purchase canteen stocks and the absence of invalid foods many of the sick were wasting away through their inability to eat the unappetizing meals, comprised in the main of rice.

Although some improvement was noticed in the health of the convalescent men only 200 men could be provided for the Engineers.

On 15th July Fukuda intimated that he would issue an additional bag of rice to permit the Convalescent Section being increased to 300 men, but immediately demanded a further 70 men for road work. It was pointed out the discharges from the Convalescent Section the previous day were insufficient to meet this new demand. Fukuda then said that the number required must be made up from men in the Malaria wards who were coming to the end of their ten-day treatment period. In this matter he was quite adamant and to Major Johnston he made it clear that the camp could expect severe punishment if the numbers were not forthcoming.

Next morning only 212 men were handed over to the Engineers, a deficiency of 38. The Senior Medical Officer and his assistants started work as soon as it was light to re-classify the men so that only the fittest would be called upon to work. Actually, the balance of 38 men were standing by throughout the morning waiting for the Engineers or the Administrative Troops to take them out to work.

At about mid-day Lt-Col Kappe, Majors Hunt and Johnston were summoned to I.J.A. Headquarters where they found Fukuda in a raging temper because his orders had not been carried out. Owing to being confined to bed with malaria since his arrival in the camp Lt-Col Kappe had not had previous dealings with this I.J.A. officer but it did not take him long to appreciate the difficulties which the other two officers had had to encounter.

Fukuda commenced his tirade with the remark that it was Japan's intention to become friendly with Australia after the war but the senior officers were doing all they could to antagonise the Japanese Army by refusing to carry out orders. He said that if he ordered that 1,000 men would go to work they would go despite any protests which we would make – the Japanese Engineers were prepared to die and the prisoners also must be prepared to sacrifice their lives for the railway. He went on to threaten that not only would the Camp Commander and his Staff be punished but all men in the camp would be made to suffer for the disobedience of his orders. Their own particular punishment was to consist of being made to stand in a fire.

It was explained to Fukuda that it had not been possible to examine the men the previous night owing to the lack of any lights and that medical re-classification had to wait until daylight. This quietened him to some extent but he pointed out that the construction of the railway had to go on without delay as it was required for operational purposes and had to be finished within a certain time at all costs, irrespective of the loss of lives of British and Australian prisoners. He said that it was of no use our quoting the articles of the Geneva Convention as our own people had offended against it by the sinking of hospital ships and anti-Axis Forces, and by running down civilian internees with steam rollers. If necessary, he concluded, the men would be required to work 3 to 4 days on end without rest.

There can be little doubt that the pressure for more men was being applied by somebody higher up. The I.J.A. would not or could not see that by forcing men to work before they were completely recovered the ultimate effect was to dry up the resources of available manpower.

During a fortnight the health situation had improved somewhat. On 13th July the total of men in hospital, including 142 in Convalescent Depot, was 1,493, made up as follows:

Cholera	28
Malaria	652
Dysentery	337
Beri Beri	114
Skin	176
Miscellaneous	44

By the 27th, the Convalescent Depot figure had increased to 300 and the number in hospital proper had been reduced to 1,066, an improvement of 129. Nevertheless, the number of men being sent to work from the Convalescent Depot was between 70 and 80 daily although the I.J.A. were given to understand that more men were coming from this source.

The reason for this was that the men from the Convalescent Depot were grouped into a special working party and given supposedly lighter work and better treatment. In any event, they were returned to camp a good deal earlier than working parties previously. With the increase in the recovery rate of hospital patients it was now possible to retain men in the Convalescent Depot for a few extra days, and to the health of these men these days were invaluable.

The disbandment of Lower Songkurai Camp and the establishment of the Burma Hospital were two projects which arose again towards the end of the month. With regard to the latter, Major Hunt, at twenty minutes notice, was ordered on 24th July to accompany Col Banno to inspect the new hospital.

On 26th July orders were given for the move of 300 to Upper Songkurai Camp. Lt-Col Kappe requested that in view of the state of the roads and the condition of the men who would necessarily have to carry heavy loads, the move be postponed until the condition of the road had improved. This request, strange to say, was approved. It was understood that all the personnel of this camp other than those destined for the Burma Hospital would be transferred to Upper Songkurai Camp.

The summary of the medical position in this camp during July is given hereunder. The figures for each period have been averaged.

Week ending:

	7 July	14 July	21 July	28 July
I.J.A. Works – Engineers	259	196	306	375
Hospital	1382	1464	1341	1265
Camp duties including				
Hospital Staff	249	228	208	214
Strength	1890	1888	1856	1854

Diseases:
Cholera   0.9%
Dysentery   24.0%
Malaria   38.5%
Beri Beri   7.7%
Ulcers & Skin   11.4%
Miscellaneous   4.5%
Convalescents   13.0%

Throughout this report where such figures as the above are quoted it must be appreciated that they represent only one disease per man. In actual fact a very great number of the men were suffering simultaneously from more than one illness at the same time, e.g., dysentery and malaria, or malaria and ulcers; beri beri in some form was always present.

Upper Songkurai Camp – No. 3

The situation which existed at this camp during July can be described as satisfactory when compared with those prevailing at the British Camps to the north and south of it.

After being guarded by only one or two soldiers since arrival in May, a distinct change took place as a result of the officers' escape from Songkurai Camp, an officer and his platoon of 33 men marching in to guard some 350 prisoners. The Officer-in-Charge in many ways was the most reasonable Japanese encountered to date and took a reasonable view of the health situation.

Although powerless to do anything towards obtaining medical supplies etc. he apparently had a good working arrangement with the local Engineers and sick men were not forced out to work. Working conditions were severe but there were few incidents if any involving brutal treatment. Rations were better here than in any other camp with the result that the general condition of the men was good and their morale was high.

Why there was a discrepancy between the ration scale in the several camps is not understood since all were under the same I.J.A. Administration and men were all doing more or less the same type of work. It was found that it was not always due to the fact that each camp was under a separate group of Engineers – in one particular case better issues of food and greater variation in articles of food were obtainable through the energy and good work of the I.J.A. Quartermaster.

About 20th July, the Camp Commander was informed that the hours of work were to be increased. Breakfast was issued at 0600 hours and the men were handed over to the Engineers at 0745 hours, a quarter of an hour before dawn. The average time of return to camp was 1930 hours, about half an hour before dark. Work now was pile driving for the railway bridges and was particularly arduous especially for men suffering from diarrhoea and other stomach troubles.

Up to the arrival of the first party from Lower Songkurai Camp on 28th July there had been no increase in the sick figures since the beginning of the month, and in point of fact there had been a slight decrease and the number of dangerously ill and seriously ill in hospital was very small. The work party strength remained at a figure between 90 and 100, i.e., about 27%. The fulfilment of this requirement meant a reduction of an average of 10 men daily engaged on camp and hospital duties. Even taking this reduction into account the percentage of men available for maintenance works in the camp was 50% higher than that allowed in Lower Songkurai Camp.

The following average daily figures summarise the medical position in this camp during the month of July:

	1-10 July	11-20 July	21-31 July
I.J.A. Work – Engineers	98	96	128
Hospital Patients	200	203	229
Camp duties including Hospital Staff	81	78	73
Strength	379*	377*	430*

* Includes officers engaged on camp works.

Ponds' Battalion

On 3rd July the party arrived at Takanun and preparations were made for the construction of the camp which was to be the base for Lt-Col Pond's Party for two months.

For the whole period of the march the rations had been as follows:

Rice – an average of 12 ozs per man per day
Meat – four issues which averaged at 2.1 ozs per man per day
Vegetables – one issue on 30th June of 8 ozs
Whitebait – one issue on 20th June of 0.4 ozs

The medical position at the end of the previous month showed that out of 636 men 458 were classified as sick under the following headings:

Cholera	10
Malaria	135
Ulcers	110
Dysentery & Diarrhoea	105
Beri Beri	35
Diptheria	3
Miscellaneous	60

Of the balance, there was not one man who was not suffering from complete exhaustion. They appeared to be in a pitiful condition. With bodies like skeletons, they were clothed in dirty, torn and ill-fitting shorts and shirts. 150 men were without boots, few men with socks. The hats of those who had them were old and perished, many heads were shaved and the exigencies of the march had made face shaving a rarity.

In this state the men reached a site selected by Lieut Murayama at Takanun on a bamboo covered hillside sloping to a tributary of the main river. The total area allotted for sleeping, cookhouses, latrines and hospital was about 65 by 75 yards and this included a portion which was too steep to permit of the erection of tents. Half a day was allowed for the clearing and preparation of the site and on 4th July the first working party was ordered out to work.

It is from this date onwards that attention must be paid to the full significance of what constituted a "working day". In no country in the world, however low its labour standards, could an employer subject his employees to such treatment. One can only wonder how the human frame could take the punishment to which it was subjected. It is worthy of note that when frantic efforts were being made to complete the railway in the scheduled time and Japanese soldiers were impressed to assist in the work, in spite of better food for months they were only capable of maintaining the pressure for one day.

The bald words "a working day" will now be examined. This examination will be deliberately detailed for in general terms it expresses the hardships suffered by working parties throughout the Force.

Reveille invariably was at 0700 hours in pitch darkness and usually in pouring rain. Mess orderlies would have to attend at the cookhouse and stagger up a slimy slope carrying heavy mess dixies of rice. Other men meanwhile would have lined up in a queue to take their turn in dipping their mess tins in boiling water for sterilisation purposes. They then would move to a second line-up to receive their rice and finally were compelled to squat or stand in the rain while consuming their ration. Immediately this was over they lined up again to wash their mess tins and be issued with their luncheon issue of rice to be carried out to work with them.

As first light appeared the medical officer would commence his sick parade and every man who had become ill overnight or required dressings for injuries, ulcers etc. attended at the R.A.P. At 0800 hours the working party fell in and efforts then had to be made to obtain extra men to bring up the numbers to the Japanese requirements, replacing those marked by the medical officer as unfit to go to work.

At 0815 hours the party moved off across a high level bridge, 80 yards long, the track being constructed of slippery logs 6″ wide. Men whose nerves were not equal to the task of negotiating this bridge were compelled to cross a low level bridge two or three feet under water. At 0830 hours a second parade of the work party was held by the Japanese, a check of numbers made and tools issued, and at the conclusion of this the men were herded off to the job about two miles away through deep mud or across sharp flint-like stones or gravel. As half the camp at this stage was without boots the journey always was a trial, stragglers being smacked on the face on arrival for lateness.

Having arrived at the job the men were divided into teams of 3 or 4, one man to pick the cutting face of the rock, one to shovel and two men to carry away the spoil in bamboo stretcher-like baskets. This last duty usually meant a carry of shale, rock or soaking clay for a distance of 50 to 75 yards through yellow oozing clay on a bed of gravel. Again men's feet suffered badly.

Almost without exception the periods of work were 50 minutes with a ten-minute break for smoking. When the men were on contract labour, which frequently as the case, the rest period was often used by dysentery and diarrhoea cases to obey nature's call. The break for lunch was taken from 1330 hours to 1500 hours, being reduced to one hour for the last months work on the railway. It was extraordinary during the first six weeks of this camp how frequently meal hours and torrential downpours coincided.

The start work signal for the afternoon heralded speculation as to what would be the knock-off hour, but speculation was useless. Last light at this time of the year was in the vicinity of 2115 hours and usually this was the time for cessation of work. Then followed the collection and counting of tools and baskets, checking of men and the order to return to camp. To many men this return journey was one of the greatest trials of the day. Exhausted from work, feet cut and sore, clothes wet and cold, they set out to pick or feel their way in the dark through two miles of mud, including a balancing task across three bridges.

Arriving in camp at about 2215 hours, again they would line up to sterilise their mess gear and then draw their evening meal of rice and jungle-leaf-flavoured water. The more fortunate would cluster around a fire and then grope their way down to the river to wash off the day's mud and sweat. Another sick parade and dressings completed, the men were able, usually by 2300 hours, to don a damp shirt (if such an article still was in their possession), roll themselves in a blanket, probably damp, and lie down under a rotted, dripping tent.

How much sleep a man got depended on the state of his bowels and how many times he was disturbed by his neighbour in the tent visiting the latrines. 0700 hours the next day would see a repetition of this programme. No day was set aside for rest and the only chance that a man had of a day in camp was to satisfy the medical officer that he was completely unfit for work. That in itself was no easy task for the reason that the Japanese would indicate the number of men required for the following day and without exception this number was far in excess of any reasonable demand, so that the medical officer could only excuse a man at the expense of some other man slightly less ill.

A day off in camp, however, was by no means a day of rest. The first task usually consisted of the scrubbing of clothes. Soap was non-existent, the river muddy and mud and sweat from a fortnight's work did not make this task easy. By 1000 hours camp duties had been allotted, such as drain digging, maintenance and digging of fresh latrines, cutting and carrying of bamboo for construction of floors for the ever-increasing hospital patients, firewood fatigues and possibly the most nerve racking of all, cremation parties.

Seldom a day passed without a death occurring, sometimes there were five or six, and owing to the heavy rain fires might have to be maintained for 6 or 7 hours before the bodies would be sufficiently disposed of. Water parties to the river, particularly for the I.J.A. cookhouse also were added. Finally, it was the custom for any Japanese private to walk into the camp and order a party of 10 or 20 men for any particular job which had been assigned to him by his N.C.O.

The result of all these fatigues having to be done with very limited labour available was that the men generally were reluctant, in spite sometimes of genuine illness, to be excused by the medical officer from railway construction work. Furthermore, there was the risk that an I.J.A. medical inspection would be held at which Murayama himself would carry out the examination and in order to bring up the working figures to the required strength he would drive even the sickest man out of camp. It is literally true that only men who were close to death were allowed to remain in camp. It is equally true that deaths of many men were caused, or at least accelerated by this system of purge.

The above paragraphs endeavour to illustrate the basis of working conditions. Superimposed on these conditions, however, the following matters made life still more difficult. As mentioned above, the men were divided at work into teams of 3 or 4. These teams were told at the commencement of the day's work that each team would be responsible for carrying anything up to 700 baskets for the day. Four fit men if in close proximity to the dumping pit might succeed sometimes in fulfilling the task, but only to be told that a fresh contract had been assigned to them.

On the other hand, it needed only one sick man in the team to retard operations with the result that Nippon guards with bamboo sticks in their hands would stand over the men and strike them as they passed. Another difficulty which the men had to face on these contract jobs was the poor conditions of the tools provided. Baskets broke hourly, involving delay in repairing them, shovels in many cases were made of unused petrol drums and bent double, picks were badly blunted and made little impression on stone, tool handles were made of timber out from the jungle and caused blisters and cut hands.

The next and perhaps the most serious matter was the number of hours allocated for work. Eight to ten hours manual labour on a solid diet for seven days a week would test a professional labourer. The majority of these men, however, had never done manual work in their lives; they were men who had lived on a basic diet of rice for 16 months and now on a starvation diet were being compelled to work a minimum of 13 hours a day while suffering from malaria, diarrhoea or ulcers.

On 27th July the first news was received that hours would be lengthened. Without apparent reason the knock-off time was made 2240 hours. By 13th August the hours were inhuman. For four days in succession the hours of work were from 0800 to 0240 on the following day; 1000 to 2200; 0800 to 2300 and finally 0800 to 0245 hours.

With regard to the working of officers, the position in the Pond Battalion differed from the others. From the commencement officers were required to accompany the men to work or a reason given as to why they remained in camp. When work started at Takanun officers were ordered out to work in special parties but on a slightly lighter contract basis. As time went on sickness reduced the number of officers sufficiently to make their portion of work negligible, and they were utilized solely for supervising the men or acting as tally clerks for the number of baskets carried by the men. Suspicions (perhaps not unjustified) that the tally was too favourable to the men stopped this practice, although at one stage Korean guards desirous of returning to camp early frequently connived at additions to the tally much to the annoyance of the Japanese Engineers.

About the time that tallying ceased the number of men collapsing at work increased alarmingly, and the reaction of the Engineers correspondingly became more dangerous. A new policy therefore was adopted by certain of the officers who were regularly out at work. If a member of one of the men's teams suffering beyond all reasonable endurance from malaria, diarrhoea, ulcers or jungle fever appealed to the guard to be allowed to rest he invariably was refused. An officer then would volunteer to fill the man's place in the team and a grudging acquiescence would be granted. As time went on the guard discovered that these officers were capable of equalling the men's work and they became satisfied that the output of the team was maintained. At odd periods compulsory officers' working parties were ordered but these seldom lasted more than a few days.

Returning to the story of the position during the month of July, a survey of the health situation is as follows:

	10th July	*20th July*	*30th July*
Cholera	15	51	56*
Malaria	235	140	90*
Ulcers	32	25	20*
Dysentery & Diarrhoea	125	186	107*
Beri Beri	35	27	22*
Miscellaneous	22	23	17*
Fit and sick working	211	202	179*

* The drop in figures at this date was due to the fact that on 26th July the first batch of 70 very sick were despatched by boat down the river to Kanburi Hospital.

Chapter 7

Re-Organization and Conditions during the Height of the Monsoon Period, August–September and during October

From the scanty information given by the I.J.A. it appears that the original plan for the re-organisation of the camps was the closing of Lower Songkurai (A.I.F.) and No. 5 Camp (British) and for the concentration of all British personnel at Songkurai and all A.I.F. (except Pond's battalion) at Upper Songkurai Camps. Nieke Headquarters Camp also was to close down except for a few medical personnel and a few drivers and mechanics.

It should be borne in mind that at this time two-thirds of the men in all camps were hospital patients and many of the men were so ill that they had been classified as unfit for the journey to Burma Hospital. Consequently, at Lower Songkurai Camp, and it is safe to say at Nieke also, requests were made as soon as the moves were mooted for the provision of motor transport for the transfer of the very sick.

These requests were not met, neither were those for the use of one or two lorries for the cartage of heavy camp stores which had to be moved to the new locations. This meant that the seriously ill would have to be stretcher borne and the camp stores manhandled. When it is realized that every day a convoy of empty ration lorries passed the camp on their return journey to Burma it is almost unbelievable that such a state of affairs could be permitted by soldiers of a nation which claimed to be civilized.

Even if there had been no chance of obtaining permission to employ the ration lorries, it is to be remembered that at Col Banno's Headquarters there were always one or two lorries and an ambulance in commission. These vehicles with many others had been brought from Changi for the use of the Force.

Movement commenced on 28th July, the first party from No. 1 Camp comprising 7 Officers and 293 Other Ranks. With the exception of a very few fit men this party was made up of sick and patients from the Convalescent Depot. Apart from their loads of personal gear, which admittedly were not as heavy as when the Force left Banpong, the men were obliged to carry a proportion of camp equipment including heavy cast-iron rice boilers, blankets, large mosquito nets, cooking utensils and other minor items.

It may not appear that a distance of 5 miles would present any hardship to the fit men but when it is remembered that the road literally was a ribbon of mud it is not surprising that even the strongest of the men were in an exhausted condition when they arrived at No. 3 Camp, after having taken five hours to complete the journey. The sick and convalescents had to be helped in by their comrades, many in the last stages of exhaustion. The nett result was that 173 men of the 300 had to be admitted to hospital at once. Some were never to leave the hospital alive.

As was the case with all other parties to arrive at this camp, the Camp Commander had not been informed of the numbers expected or the time and date of their arrival.

On 1 August, a further 500 were ordered to move from No. 1 to No. 3 Camp. This party, according to Lieut Fukuda, was to include all the remaining fit men with the exception of about 50 who had been selected as the maintenance personnel for the Burma Hospital. This order was subsequently cancelled and in lieu 300 were ordered to move to No. 2 Camp and the remaining 200 to No. 3 Camp. The reason given for this change is interesting. The I.J.A. had decided to mix the British troops and the Australians with the idea of improving the poor position then existing in British Camps, where the death rates were alarmingly high. The higher morale, standard of hygiene and physical fitness of the A.I.F. would, it was thought, act as an encouragement to the personnel of Nos. 2 and 5 Camps, both of which were in a deplorable condition. In No. 2 Camp, 8-10 British troops were dying daily whereas in No. 1 Camp only 8 A.I.F. deaths occurred in July.

To add to the difficulties, it was known that the hospital conditions at No. 2 Camp were bad and that the accommodation was overtaxed. Major Johnston, who had been left in charge of No. 1 Camp when Lt-Col Kappe left to command No. 3 Camp, decided to move the seriously ill to No. 3 Camp instead of to No. 2. The additional stretcher carry of 3 kilometres over slippery and hilly country placed an added strain on the semi-fit stretcher bearers and on the patients of the second party, which was made up of 7 Officers and 209 Other Ranks. Of the latter only 100 were fit to carry loads and these had to be detailed to carry the 16 stretcher cases and to assist the 94 men who were just fit to walk (stumble or crawl would better express their condition).

As the party was assembling it was found that three of the stretcher cases were too ill to make the trip and they had to be re-admitted to hospital. One died within a few minutes and another a day or two later. One of the men carried to No. 3 Camp died of exhaustion within a day of his arrival and many of the others who made the journey died subsequently.

On this journey there was hardly a man, fit or otherwise, who was not burdened with a load of camp stores. The ordeal would have tested men in the best physical condition and it is no wonder, therefore, that even many of the fit became casualties and subsequently died through being forced out to work without an opportunity of resting after their ordeal. Of this party 109 were admitted to hospital directly on arrival.

This act of barbaric cruelty could have been avoided had the slightest sympathy been shown by Lieut Fukuda or had some degree of liaison existed between neighbouring Japanese administrations.

On the same day Major Tracey moved to No. 2 Camp with 7 Officers, 143 Fit men and 147 hospital patients. This party suffered but not quite to the same extent as those who moved further on. They were joined by a second party of 300 A.I.F. on 4th August and by several hundred British and Australians from Nieke. On 5th August 32 Australians from No. 1 Camp marched to No. 3 followed by 82 more on 7th August.

All that remained now at No. 1 Camp were the ?00 [illegible] sick destined for Burma Hospital and their maintenance party of 50. Actually only 277 of this group were moved to Burma, the balance being transferred to No. 2 Camp under similar conditions to the other parties. As this move did not take place until late in September, No. 1 Camp can be looked upon as a hospital camp from 5th August onwards.

As the huts were vacated by our troops moving north they were occupied by thousands of natives amongst whom cholera had broken out. The camp escaped another epidemic only by the prompt action of the camp and medical staff but only after a few men had contracted the disease. Unfortunately as it will be seen later one was a member of the party transferred to No. 3 Camp whose activities during the months of August and September will now be narrated.

Upper Songkurai Camp – August

In addition to the four parties of Australians from No. 1 Camp totalling about 650 all ranks, No. 3 Camp was increased by 310 British troops from No. 5 Camp and about 360 from Nieke.

By 8th August the strength of the camp was approximately 1,690 all ranks, 670 were British troops and 1,020 Australians. The former were in poorer condition than the Australians from No. 1 Camp and an estimate of their state can readily be formed from that which already has been told. No. 5 Camp had been through a particularly gruelling time since its establishment in May. Of the original 600, 200 had died during the cholera epidemic which was simultaneous with the other outbreaks mentioned earlier.

The treatment at the hands of the Engineers had been severe, with many sick being forced out to work under terrible conditions for days on end. The men from Nieke, too, almost without exception had been discharged from hospital on the days on which they had been forced to march the 16 kilometres over appalling roads.

The increase in strength in this camp was attended by considerable confusion brought about by the customary failure of the I.J.A. Administration to make the simplest preparations in advance. What had been needed was a gang of coolies to put the huts in an habitable condition by roofing and strengthening of the floors and to construct extra latrines and put in drainage.

Instead, only two or three Burmese were employed on roofing with the result that the demand for accommodation always exceeded the supply. As was to be expected Camp Headquarters were not permitted to withdraw any men from Engineer work to put the huts in a sanitary condition, let alone do anything to the buildings themselves.

The low morale of the sick men from No. 5 Camp and Nieke Camp received no stimulant when they saw for the first time the dilapidated quarters which they were compelled to occupy and when the flooring of bay after bay collapsed under the weight of sick men who had been crowded into them.

As an indication of the position the following figures for 7th August are quoted:

	Strength	Sick	Engineer Work	Hospital Staff	Cooks	Other Duties
British	646	492	110	4	-	40}*
A.I.F.	937	403	390	51	41	52}*
Total	1583	895	500	55	41	92

* Includes 55 Officers.

This absorbed all the reasonably fit men in the camp, yet soon after the work party marched out that morning a demand was made for a further 30 men to cut and bring in bamboo for hut construction. Protests were made on the ground that this would adsorb all the administrative staff and men engaged on vital sanitation works, drainage, etc. but the only answer given was a demand for an additional 50 to erect a fence between the camp and coolie lines. It was pointed out that men would have to be drawn from hospital for this work but no alleviation was granted and men in the final stages of malaria treatment were put on to constructing a barrier which was a fence in name only.

The fact that the camp was in a shocking condition did not impress the I.J.A. one iota. The latrines were still flooded by the incessant rain, one had broken its banks and a filthy stream oozed through the camp area and passed under the floors of the huts occupied by the hospital, the outside and even the inside of the huts was a quagmire and the cookhouse still was inadequate for present needs.

Against all this, protests couched in the strongest possible terms were made by Lt-Col Kappe and Major Stevens, Senior Medical Officer A.I.F., who by this time had arrived to reinforce the small medical team of only two officers and less than 20 trained nursing orderlies.

The whole position pertaining in the camp had been further deteriorated by the arrival of Lieut Fukuda and his notorious assistant Toyama. Mr. Korayasu, the I.J. Interpreter, had been left in charge of the remnants of No. 1 Camp and did not come forward until late in September. This was most unfortunate as it placed the control of the camp literally in the hands of Toyama who possessed a smattering of English, a factor which was to prove a danger to the troops rather than an advantage.

This Gunsoku [Sergeant] wielded some considerable influence with Fukuda which could only be explained by the troops in the grossest terms. From the experiences of his attitude and actions already gained at No. 1 Camp nothing but unjust treatment now could be expected. Lieut Fukuda's first order was to the effect that no Englishman was to be employed in the cookhouse or on any other camp duties so that every available man in the British battalion could be sent to Engineer work despite his age or physical condition. As there were about 70 fit men only in the whole 670, it therefore became necessary to protect the weaker men by keeping them in hospital until they had recovered sufficiently to take on heavy work. This threw a heavy strain upon the Australians and was without doubt the cause of the comparative increase in the death rate of the A.I.F. in late September and October.

The I.J.A. seemed determined to do all in their power to break the British troops and to discriminate between them and the Australians. At every turn disparaging remarks were made against the former, about their percentage of sick and their inability to provide their proportion of workers for the road and railway. By I.J.A. order amalgamation of the men in hospital was forbidden resulting in duplication in the handling of cases of a similar category by the already overworked staff. Any attempt to establish a combined organisation was frustrated by the I.J.A. refusing to allow the Camp Commander to make his own allotment of accommodation etc.

It was about this time that the Senior Medical Officer approached Lieut Fukuda on the question of hygiene and additional food particularly for the sick and submitted that unless something was done to remedy the situation a serious loss of life would ensue. The more or less favourable attitude which Lieut Fukuda had adopted towards hygiene and health in No. 1 Camp had now disappeared and his future actions were to be guided by a spirit of brutal callousness.

The formation of a Convalescent Depot, where men recovering from illness could be rested for a few days instead of being discharged direct to lines where they could be at once detected by the guards had little effect. So insistent and unreasonable were the demands for workers outside and inside the camp that only the very ill were spared.

Accommodation was overtaxed but the work of improving some of the existing huts went on at a snail's pace – yet at the same time all speed was demanded from the sick men who had been called out to construct new quarters for the Korean Guard. The average number of men accommodated in each 10 feet by 10 feet bay now was 14 and the same position appertained in the hospital where sick men were lying shoulder to shoulder.

On the night of 9th August Lieut Fukuda demanded 550 working men for the Engineers for the 10th. Figures were produced to show that the number of sick was nearing 1,000 and that the British battalion could provide only a little more than 100 out of their strength of 650. This infuriated Fukuda who then demanded that the British battalion would provide 150 men and the Australians 400.

A further examination revealed that by taking every man in camp other than cooks and by including 10 officers – a figure again not permitted by the Engineers – only 522 could be provided. This was pointed out to Fukuda in a stormy interview in which Fukuda remained adamant. The Camp Commander then asked permission to reduce the British quota at the expense of more A.I.F. who although ill were in slightly better heart then the Englishmen. This also was refused and Fukuda reiterated that his orders would stand.

The Camp Commander then asked that his protest against the sending out to work of seriously ill British troops be forwarded to Col Banno. Toyama, who had acted as a most unsatisfactory interpreter, translated this request whereupon Lt-Col Kappe was struck. Knowing that the refusal to carry out these orders would only result in further reprisals steps were taken at midnight to classify the "not so Sicks". This heart-breaking situation was explained to the men who received the information stoically although many must have known that it would be only a matter of hours on the morrow before the Engineers would be compelled to return them to camp in a collapsing state and fit only for re-admission to hospital. In the weeks to come dozens of men were returned to camp as unfit for work yet the demands for the increased numbers persisted.

On 10th August the sorry spectacle of nearly 200 Light Duty and No Duty men being forced almost to crawl to work in the pouring rain was witnessed and yet that same day Fukuda demanded that the next day 200 British troops would be included in the work party which was to be further increased to 600.

There was an instance on 10th August where a man who had collapsed on the job was not permitted to return to camp and was forbidden to take his mid-day rice because he had not worked. Instances of this form of brutality by the Engineers on this section of the railway fortunately were rare although the tasks which the men were called upon to perform were severe and became worse as August and September progressed.

On the same day, the 10th, another calamity was to befall the camp. One of the men who had collapsed at work and been returned to hospital was diagnosed as a cholera case. He was one of a party which left No. 1 Camp after the outbreak of the disease there amongst the coolies. It was not until the middle of September after some 150 men had been isolated and nearly 50 had died that the epidemic was beaten.

The area selected for the isolation hospital on this occasion was a small cleared space of low-lying ground on the river bank, where the mud was ankle deep and the only fixed accommodation a small hut capable of holding no more than 30 patients. The remainder of the personnel placed in isolation had to be quartered in tents and under tent-flies which invariably leaked. No fit men were freed from Engineer work to assist the sick in providing stagings to keep them from the muddy ground and all duties except nursing had to be performed by the personnel in isolation.

Requests for more serviceable tents and the release of men from work to improve the area and even for a few additional tools all met the same fate, and the sick were left to their miserable plight. Except for numerous glass red tests and the supply of vaccine two days after the first outbreak there was a heartless indifference on the part of the I.J.A. to the sufferings of the dying men. Needless to say Lieut Fukuda at no time visited the cholera quarters and informed the officer in charge that he was held personally responsible for the outbreak of cholera. With no competent or reliable interpreter available it was not possible for Lt-Col Kappe to convey what he thought of the whole proceedings and that this was the best example of "passing the buck" which so far had been experienced.

Upon this fresh outbreak of cholera being reported the I.J.A. medical personnel arrived at the camp with amazing promptitude and carried out a glass red test of all personnel. Among those classified by the I.J.A. test as cholera carriers was Capt Juttner, one of the only three medical officers in the camp and this threw an added strain on Major Stevens and his assistant, Capt Wilson, R.A.M.C. Some valuable and much needed help was obtained from the services of Assistant Surgeon James, Indian Medical Service who had been sent up from No. 2 Camp.

The following is a summary of this outbreak:

	Patients Admitted	Carriers Admitted	Deaths in Isolation	Cholera other Causes	Fatality Rate
British	48	25	37	1	79.17%
Australian	21	65	10	3	57.14%

Mention must be made here of the splendid services rendered by NX17742 Pte Murray, D.E., A.A.M.C. who was in sole charge of the nursing during this and the previous cholera outbreak at this camp. Particular mention of this man's services will be made later.

During August the camp was a living "Hell" for all its occupants. Every small matter was exaggerated and made the reason for an "incident" by the I.J.A. As an example of this the following particular instances are given:

1. Two Englishmen were observed throwing away some scraps of rice; they stated later that they were too ill to eat the unappetizing food. This was taken by the Korean Quartermaster as indicating that the British troops were getting too much food and orders were issued to the effect that the rations for the British battalion were to be reduced by one-third. In actual fact, this was merely a counter on the part of the I.J.A. to protests that the troops were starving on the present ration which was of very poor quality – boxed meat issued at this stage was alive with maggots and more often than not 80 per cent had to be buried.

2. At times, and as a matter of necessity, a risk was taken, and the meat cooked and when brought to the boil the maggots were skimmed off the top before the meat was served. By adjustment, the working men in the British battalion continued to receive the same scale as the Australian heavy workers but it was some days later, after repeated requests had been made, before a portion of the reduction in rice issue was restored.

3. On 30 August, a British officer was observed speaking to his Commanding Officer who was passing the camp on foot en route to the Burma Hospital. For this 'crime' – no orders had been issued against speaking to British personnel on the road – the officer was tied up with ropes to the stump of a tree outside I.J.A.

Headquarters for some hours in full view of the troops and the hundreds of coolies in the vicinity.

4. On the following day, a pick could not be found after finish of camp work. It was obvious that it had been removed by another section of the Japanese quartered in the camp, presumably in error. When the matter was reported to Toyama, who was temporarily in charge of the camp, he ordered that unless the pick was found overnight rations for the whole camp including the sick would be stopped until the pick was handed in. At 2330 hours Lt-Col Kappe, the O.C. British Troops and Capt Swartz were taken to the I.J.A. Headquarters and arraigned before Toyama. After much discussion and protests against starving the hospital patients had been lodged, Lt-Col Kappe stated that on behalf of the Australians who had been using this particular tool that day he would take full responsibility.

On this Toyama reduced the punishment by stopping only the meals of the officers and personnel on camp duties, a search being ordered to be carried out at Reveille next day. Next morning this was done by all excepting a few sick officers and the medical officers. Observing these officers, Toyama screamed in rage and the three officers referred to above were taken to the Japanese quarters and spoken to at great length on the subject of obedience.

Efforts to explain that his orders had been carried out were of no avail. As the Camp Commander had personally taken the responsibility for the matter he had no option but to kneel on the ground when he was ordered. This humiliation was shared by the other two officers who agreed soto voce that to refuse would only bring trouble on the heads of the men who so far had been spared. The missing pick was found a few minutes later, peculiarly enough in the area which had been diligently searched throughout the night and morning. After Toyama had apologised "for all the trouble" the incident closed.

5. This Gunsoku was himself prominent and offensive during a search of the camp by Japanese Military Police. Whereas the search by the latter was carried out thoroughly and quietly with the minimum damage to men's gear, the Gunsoku seemed to delight in throwing personal effects on to the muddy ground and

walking over men's scanty pieces of bedding in his muddy boots. His roaring and yelling commenced at dawn and continued until midnight. It is no wonder that the nerves of everybody in the camp were at breaking point.

Apart from the severity of the demands for road and railway work, Lieut Fukuda had demanded men for the construction of new huts and kitchen for the Korean Guards and for the construction of a fence which fronted the camp only. Threats now began to be made that unless demands for working parties were met in full the whole camp including the sick and dying would have to camp in the jungle without tents in order to make way for thousands of coolies who would have to be called in so that the section of the railway in this area could be completed on time.

On 16th August after every demand seemed to have been met even to the satisfaction of the Japanese, 50 men were demanded from the hospital. This was refused. A stormy incident occurred when the guards entered the hospital and attempted to intimidate the sick by striking the flooring close to the men's bodies. The Camp Commander ordered the men not to budge and protested on humanitarian grounds. Toyama then appeared and threatened all forms of punishment and stated that unless 50 men were out of the hospital within five minutes the whole camp would be placed on half-rations and that the guards would forcibly eject men picked at random.

In a hurried conference the Senior Medical Officer advised that more harm would ensue if the present meagre ration was reduced by 50% and if the guards and not he made the selection of the men required for work and in these circumstances 50 patients in the final stages of Malaria treatment were selected. Yet another determined effort to save the sick from unwarranted brutality had proven unsuccessful.

The number of sick, including those "sick in lines", passed the 1,000 mark on 13th August and steadily grew to a maximum of 1,124 on 17th August. Up to 1st September inclusive the daily number of sick averaged 1,050.

The hospital states for the period 3rd to 31st August are summarised below:

A.I.F.					
August	*3rd*	*10th*	*17th*	*24th*	*31st*
Dysentery	29	56	53	50	80
Malaria	91	110	122	98	91
Beri Beri*	25	78	103	119	103
Pneumonia	-	-	-	-	4
Tropical Ulcers & Skin	50	128	134	125	138
Cholera (including Carriers)	-	3	64	68	75
Miscellaneous	1	3	18	25	24
Total	204	378	494	485	515

British Troops					
Dysentery		176	125	96	114
Malaria		129	116	88	119
Beri Beri*		77	76	64	63
Tropical Ulcers & Skin		115	97	98	98
Cholera (incl carriers)		-	26	75	64
Miscellaneous		19	18	21	21
Total		516	458	442	479

Deaths for period – A.I.F. 23, British Troops 42.

Total number in hospital 31st August – 994.

Sick for whom no accommodation available – 35.

Proportion of camp strength sick – 63.5%.

* The S.M.O. reported that 100% of the camp was suffering from Beri Beri to some degree.

It can be seen from above that despite the untiring devotion to duty of the medical officers and hospital staff the situation was most serious. The conditions inside the hospital were dreadful. The stench from the ulcer and dysentery wards was well-nigh unbearable. Sick men were lying shoulder to shoulder on a rough bamboo staging, some without a covering other than an old bag which the I.J.A. had issued. The roof of the dysentery ward leaked badly; repeated requests for the replacement of the attap had all met with indifference and it was a pitiable sight to see some 70 odd patients huddled together in the passageway every time it rained at all heavily, their bedding and what little other gear they possessed having been hurriedly stacked on one side where it was dry.

The threat that the camp would be invaded by natives was borne out on 19th August when a complete line of huts had to be evacuated to make room for them. To overcome the great shortage of accommodation which resulted some of the huts were double-decked, but the position requiring from 14 to 16 men to occupy each bay instead of 8 for which they had been designed still remained.

Mainly due to the work of one or two hygiene N.C.O.s and the spare officers, some progress was made by the end of the month in the digging of new latrines, the erection of a new kitchen and the building of a few "corduroy" paths through the camp area.

The arrival of thousands of natives presented a fresh danger from disease. Between their huts and the fence erected to prevent contact with them the coolies threw scrap rice and defaecated and urinated at will. Flies began to breed prolifically and the stench was indescribable, as was the noise which emanated from the huts for the 24 hours of the day, depriving the sick and working men alike of much needed sleep. Requests to Lieut Fukuda to have this No-Man's Land cleared was only met with the answer that the coolies came under the control of the Engineers and that he could do nothing. A particularly obnoxious latrine had been dug within 10 yards of the point from which the camp had to draw water, whilst also above this was the Japanese guards' washing point and kitchen. It almost seemed at times that the I.J.A. would have been pleased to see the death rate so increase that their worry of guarding the prisoners would be removed.

Working conditions throughout the month were particularly arduous. A three-mile walk to the job first over rough stones and then through slippery jungle path with no boots was a heavy enough strain on the unfit men without the task of digging a deep cutting which required three separate removals of the earth owing to the depth of the cutting. Other men were engaged on bridge construction and the handling of heavy timbers for long hours.

As the days went on, the time that the men returned to camp was getting later and later and by 31st August it was 2230 hours before they came in for their evening meal. At dark a guard was placed on the section of the creek used for ablution and as this guard remained on duty until 0800 hours, by which time the men had moved out to work again, many personnel went for days without a wash except that obtained in pools on the side of a road.

The rations for the month were poor and quite inadequate for the workers and indigestible by the very sick. Oil, towgay etc which would have provided the sick with more appetizing food was not issued nor were purchases of these articles from Nieke Village permitted, although supplies were available there.

The average daily ration was Beans 2.5 ozs, Salt 0.0024 ozs, Whitebait 0.75 ozs, Boxed Meat 2 ozs (less than ½ oz reached the men because of its maggoty condition), Rice 24 ozs for Engineer workers, 20 ozs for camp workers and 16 ozs for hospital patients. An attempt was made to reduce the effects of Beri-Beri by the collection of green leaves from the area near the camp. These were boiled into a stew and given to special cases.

The first news of the officers who had escaped from No.2 Camp was received on 27th August when a party under Lieut Fukuda left to bring in the four survivors of the original party of nine. Fiendish delight was displayed by the camp guards when they informed the camp that the escapees were to be brought to the camp and executed.

Despite the conditions enumerated above the morale of the Australians still remained high. With a rare exception the men were determined if necessary to fight it out until they collapsed through the strain of heavy work and insufficient rations.

Upper Songkurai Camp – September

It had been hoped that by the beginning of this month the work on the railway cuttings, embankments and bridges would have been completed but despite the employment of two or three thousand Burmese natives who had arrived in the area much work yet remained to be done.

It was to be 18th September before the section of the railway in the vicinity of the camp was ready to take the sleepers and rails which, it was ascertained, were being laid down from the Burma end by special gangs drawn from "A" Force (ex Changi in April, 1942). Nor was there any respite from the monsoonal rains which had eased for a few days in the third week of August but again set in with renewed intensity and continued throughout the whole of September. The first 2½ weeks of September was the most severe period which the men in this camp had to endure.

To provide the numbers demanded each day, sick men had to be included in the working parties. Many of these were returned to camp early by the Engineers after being threatened with thrashings if they appeared at work again. Appeals were made to have the numbers reduced on the ground that defenceless men were in danger of being maltreated but the administration stated that the increased numbers had been demanded by Engineer Headquarters at Nieke and that they were powerless to intervene.

As a result of deaths the camp strength was gradually decreasing and the average sick figures was being maintained yet no relief was granted as the following figures for the period 1st-14th September will indicate:

Camp Strength	Sick	Engineer Work Parties		Camp Work Parties*	
		from lines	from Hosp	from lines	from Hosp
1,599	970	393	57	132	47

* Includes all officers and hospital staff.

Despite the apparently large number on camp works these still were inadequate for the proper care of the sick, hygiene duties, fuel collecting etc.

At the beginning of the month the workers were being handed over to the Engineers at 0730 hours (this meant Reveille at 0630 hours, first light being at 0745 hours) and were being returned to camp at varying times between 2000 hours and 2130 hours.

On 11th September Col Banno arrived at the camp accompanied by his medical officer, Lieut Tanio, who made a cursory inspection of the camp lasting less than 15 minutes. The opportunity was taken by the S.M.O. to represent the case for a reduction in the strength of outside working parties. The Japanese doctor promised that he would take up the matter with Col Banno. The situation regarding the shortage of drugs was pointed out and the S.M.O. was asked to submit a list of requirements for one month, Lieut Tanio stating that he considered the move south would have commenced by the end of that period.

Two days later, the officers in charge of working parties were informed that work on the railway earthworks and bridges had to be accelerated and accordingly the men would have to remain on the jobs until the work was completed, a period estimated at between 72 and 96 hours. On the grounds that this was a certain way of killing many men a protest was lodged with the administration by the Camp Commander who was informed that superior orders had stipulated that the railway must pass No.3 Camp by 15th September at any cost.

Heavy rain fell throughout that day and in the evening conditions became so bad that the flares by which the night work was to be performed were doused by the rain, resulting in the men being returned to camp at 2130 hours.

Next day – 14th – weather conditions were a little better and working hours much longer. The men went out to work at 0630 hours but did not return until 0230 hours the following morning. Before turning in they were ordered to parade again at 0630 hours which meant at the most three hours rest. Sixty workers had to be replaced by men from hospital, the medical officers being kept busy throughout the night examining and classifying men with the object of saving the worst cases from further hardship. Needless to say, all camp duties with the exception of cooking and nursing of the sick had to cease.

On 15th September the Camp Commander had been promised that work would cease at 1530 hours that day but it was 0200 hours on the 16th before the men staggered back into camp. The strain now, both physical and mental was terrific. Men were too exhausted even to speak and acted more as automatons than human beings. It was only the thought that the end was in sight that sustained them in these days of sheer torture.

Large numbers were being returned throughout the day with reports that on some of the jobs there were too many men engaged for the work to be carried out efficiently. Promises that unfit men would be given lighter work were not always kept. The statement made by Lieut Fukuda in July that prisoners would have to be sacrificed for the railway was proving to be only too true.

A reduction of 50 was obtained on 17th September and the men were returned by 2130 hours after 15 hours of work with practically no breaks,

On the evening of 18th September it was advised that the main work was finished and that the 19th had been declared a holiday; this was the first day's respite which the men were to enjoy since the commencement of the work in May; in fact since their departure from Changi in April, always excepting of course the days of illness spent in hospital. Quite a number had worked for an unbroken period of five weeks and a few had carried on for over six weeks without a break.

As a special gesture an issue of cigarettes was made to the workers; to those who had worked 40 days on end – 200 cigarettes; 30 days 150; 20 days 100; and 15 days 50. Earlier in the month Engineer workers had received an issue of 200, the camp workers 100, and the sick 50 cigarettes per man.

Other special issues made about this time had been 1½ bags sugar, 140 tins of milk and 86 tins margarine. The I.J.A. instructed that the latter two items were to be issued to the workers. This was disregarded, however, and the bulk handed over to the hospital in the hope of saving lives of some of the seriously and dangerously ill.

The rest period was short lived for from 20th to 26th September 400 men were out again repairing wash-aways on the embankments. Starting time had been put back to 0815 hours and the work, which had become lighter, was finishing in time for the men to return to camp in daylight. For the remainder of the month only 250 men were asked for, thereby enabling the unfit to have a chance of rest and treatment. Unfortunately for many, as the casualty lists for October and November will show, the relief was to come too late.

The relations with the administration had improved since the "pick incident" and with the arrival of Korayasu (Official I.J. Interpreter) many difficulties were avoided. A new camp Quartermaster (Tomayama) who also arrived on 25th September was making genuine efforts to improve the ration position and was meeting with some success.

However, the ration was still inadequate. For the month of September the average daily issue was:

Rice	23 ozs – sufficient rice was now issued to place all men on the same scale;
Beans	1.325 ozs;
Boxed meat	2.7 ozs – 30% had to be condemned and in normal times 50% of the remainder would have been condemned as unfit for human consumption;
Fresh meat	0.02 ozs;
Salt	0.6 ozs;
Dried fish	0.32 ozs – normally 90% would have been condemned;
Potatoes	3.7 ozs – the bulk of these were issued to outside workers.

Conditions in the hospital were extremely bad. Accommodation was overtaxed to the limit and after many protests on this score approval was given on 17th September to double-deck one hospital hut and when this was completed it was possible to accommodate some of the staff and patients in the last stages of malaria treatment on the upper decking. Nothing was done, however, to repair the roof of the dysentery ward.

No medical supplies or dressings had been issued by the I.J.A. Stocks were so limited that M & B tablets had to be reserved for pneumonia cases, charcoal was the only item given for the treatment of dysentery, no sulphur was available for the treatment of scabies which were fairly general and in most cases had become infected.

Dressings for the hundreds of ulcers had to be used for weeks on end and there were no facilities for proper sterilization. The ulcer treatment parades where the infected areas were scraped by improvised instruments were horrible sights. In several cases amputations were imperative but could not be performed because of the shortage of dressings. After a direct request had been made to I.J.A. Headquarters at Nieke by the Camp Commander two rolls of lint had been handed over.

It is known that Force Headquarters had been constantly asking for medical stores to be brought forward from the dump at Banpong but the answer given always was that the road to the south was impassable. At the same time, however, war equipment and merchandise of the Nieke shopkeepers was being brought forward in quantities by river barges which were operating as far north as Nieke village throughout the monsoon period.

The health position throughout the month can be determined from the following table:

Disease	7 Sep			14 Sep			21 Sep			30 Sep			Remarks
	E	A	T	E	A	T	E	A	T	E	A	T	
Cholera	58	76	134	11	20	31	11	21	32	–	–	–	E-English
Dysentery	105	68	173	104	98	202	95	82	177	76	73	149	A-Austn.
Malaria	117	107	224	182	98	84	92	66	158	89	88	177	T-Total
Beri Beri	66	108	174	100	112	212	107	117	224	79	103	182	
Pneumonia	–	4	4	15	15	30	15	10	25	15	10	25	British Bn strength increased by 2
Tropical Ulcers & Skin	83	143	226	80	153	233	84	156	240	105	164	269	Offrs 41 ORs ex
Miscellaneous	16	23	39	6	22	28	7	23	30	6	29	35	No. 5 Camp*
Total Hospital	445	529	974	414	504	918	411	475	886	370	467	837	
Sick in Lines						19			97				
Total Sick	445	29	974	414	504	937	411	475	983	370	467	837	
Strengths	616	986	1602	608	977	1585	634*	969	1603	609	961	157	
Deaths during period ending	10	8	18	18	17	35	37	25	62	62	43	105	

Throughout the month blasting had been carried out in the quarry adjacent to the camp. This was only 50 yards away from one of the British Hospital Wards and every day large fragments of rock were falling through the roofs of all the hospital wards and about the camp. Many patients were hit, one receiving a fractured arm and others narrowly missing being killed. Many of the sick could be seen sitting up in the bays with their heads covered and absolutely terrified.

The noise of the blasting and the danger from flying stone wracked the nerves of these poor unfortunates, many of whom were too sick to move out of range of the falling stones. Requests were made for a reduction in the blasting charges but, if anything, the intensity of the blasting increased. The only suggestion offered by the administration was to transfer the sick to another part of the camp.

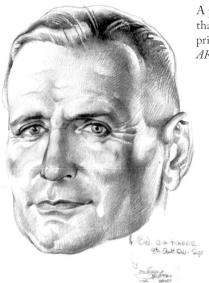

A portrait of Lieutenant Colonel Charles Henry Kappe that was drawn by Murray Griffin while both men were prisoners of war, circa 1942. (*Australian War Memorial; ART26437*)

The first truckload of Australian soldiers for 'F' Force makes it out towards the railway station marking the start of their journey in the Thai-Burmese countryside. (*Australian War Memorial; P02569.172*)

A convoy of Allied PoWs en route to Singapore railway station during the formation and initial moves of 'F' Force. At the lead of the convoy is a truck of Japanese soldiers. (*Australian War Memorial; P02569.174*)

Pictured during a break in the journey, members of 'F' Force gather by the train transporting them into Thailand to work on the Burma-Thailand railway. (*Australian War Memorial; P02569.179*)

Australian and Dutch PoWs at Tarsau in Thailand, circa 1943. All four men are suffering from beri-beri. (*Australian War Memorial; P00761.011*)

Watched by Japanese guards and engineers, prisoners are pictured manhandling sleepers at Takanun, Thailand. c.1943. (*Australian War Memorial; P00406.018*)

The starting point of the Burmese section of the Burma-Thailand railway. A Japanese soldier is pictured by the guard house near the entrance gate to the PoW camp. Thanbyuzayat camp was occupied in September 1942 and became an administration base as well as a transit camp for prisoners arriving from various sites in Burma and Java. In October 1942 it was established as a Base Hospital for seriously ill patients from up-country railway camps. (*Australian War Memorial; 045258*)

Members of an 'F' Force working party at a watering point near the border to Thailand. (*Australian War Memorial; P02569.176*)

Members of 'F' Force bathing and washing clothes on a washing platform in a stream at Kami Sonkurai Camp No.3. (*Australian War Memorial; P02569.188*)

Allied prisoners engaged on a bridge-building project somewhere on the Burma-Thailand railway. (*Australian War Memorial; 119162*)

A Japanese survey group working on the railway during 1943. (*Australian War Memorial; P00406.021*)

Australian and British prisoners laying track on the Burma-Thailand railway near Ronsi. Ronsi is approximately sixty kilometres south of Thanbyuzayat, or 354 kilometres north of Nong Pladuk, also known as Non Pladuk. (*Australian War Memorial; P00406.034*)

A stretch of track being laid by prisoners circa 1943. (*Australian War Memorial; P00406.027*)

Prisoners entering the 'bar'. The bar did not exist, and, judging by the camera in the foreground, this scene was almost certainly staged by the Japanese, probably at Thanbyazayat Base Hospital during 1943, for propaganda purposes. (*Australian War Memorial; P02569.024*)

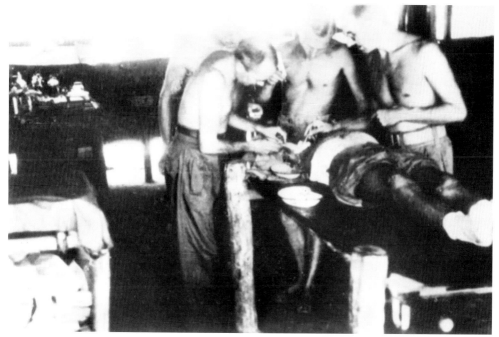

Major A.A. Moon, an Australian medical officer, at work in the hospital hut at the PoW camp at Tamuang, c.1943. (*Australian War Memorial; P00761.013*)

A punishment hole for PoWs at a camp on the railway. (*Australian War Memorial; 157872*)

A view from the train taking members of Australian soldiers of 'F' Force back to Singapore after their work on the Burma-Thailand railway had ended. (*Australian War Memorial; P02569.195*)

Morale which was particularly low amongst the British troops received a fillip on 30th September when it was announced that the move south was expected to take place in the middle of October and that Camp Headquarters had been asked to furnish a return of lying, sitting and walking cases in the camp hospital so that accommodation on the trains could be arranged.

Upper Songkurai Camp – October

After the shocking conditions that the camp had had to endure during August and September, October was to be a month of comparative peace and quiet. Now the railway was running pressure was relaxed to some extent. Unfortunately for many, relief had come too late.

Men who had been admitted to hospital during the last half of August and who had hung on gamely throughout September now were succumbing to their diseases and debility brought about by the lack of reasonable food. 149 deaths during the month reduced the camp strength from 1566 to 1417. Up to the end of September the A.I.F. deaths had only been 50% of the number sustained by the British Troops but the figures for October, viz., 86 British and 63 A.I.F. brought the proportion on a relative strength basis up to 75%, the probable cause of this increase in A.I.F. deaths has been explained previously.

Although there was no great deterioration in the health situation generally the number of sick at 31st October was 937 compared with 966 at the end of September and this despite the heavy death rate. Had the work conditions of the previous month been maintained the loss of life would have been considerably greater.

For the first week only 250 men were demanded by the Engineers but this number was increased by 100 when an Engineer Officer observed a ration party of that strength carrying rations from the abandoned No. 5 Camp. He apparently was determined that the Engineers would exact the last particle of manpower from the camp and made arrangements for the delivery of rations to be made by motor transport.

For a few days 350 men were sent out but as this figure could not be maintained without drawing men from the Convalescent Depot representations were made and the numbers were gradually reduced until during the last four days only 280 outside workers were being supplied.

This was the first occasion on which the I.J.A. administration had acceded to our protests against the demands of the Engineers. Even now over 80 men from hospital were carrying out essential duties in caring for their more sick comrades each day.

Through the efforts of Tomayama, the I.J.A. Quartermaster, the quantity and standard of the rations also improved, the average daily scale being Rice 23 ozs; Beans 2 ozs; Boxed Meat 1 oz; Fresh Meat 0.55 ozs; Potatoes 10.75 ozs; Salt 1.3 ozs. In addition, gula malacca, curry, coffee and sauce were issued in small quantities from time to time and with the aid of a few canteen supplies which now were coming to hand more appetizing meals could be provided for the sick.

For a number of reasons, none of which seemed justifiable, it had not been possible to obtain certain canteen supplies during the whole of August and September. It was most heartening, therefore, when at the beginning of October Force Headquarters at No. 2 Camp were able to purchase from Nieke on behalf of the camp such items as towgay, peanuts, oil and tinned fish. The bulk of the vitamin foods were purchased for the hospital from funds deducted from officers' pay and it now was possible to provide 250 men with a special diet.

It was only lack of supplies which prevented the increase of this number. Since the inception of the Force the officers had donated approximately half their pay to hospital funds and these by now were considerable. An amount had been transferred to the Burma Hospital but ample remained for the benefit of the sick whenever the I.J.A. authorities thought fit to provide the necessary facilities for purchase from Nieke.

It was unfortunate that after one or two deliveries supplies were stopped from leaving Nieke. No doubt a "squeeze" had been introduced, for when deliveries were resumed later in the month all prices had risen.

The inability to trade through authorized channels had the effect of driving the men to purchase minor items of tobacco etc. surreptitiously from the natives. With cholera and smallpox prevalent in the coolie camp this was dangerous, particularly as it was appreciated that any outbreak of either of these two diseases would result in movement to the south being delayed for weeks. Reluctantly orders to enforce the I.J.A. ruling that no contact was to be had with the natives had to be issued and continuous picquets and patrols had to be instituted.

The stoppage of canteen supplies provided the guards with an opportunity to profiteer in the sale of tinned milk, meat, vegetables etc. with which they had been issued in fair quantity. Realizing that the troops had been starved for months and were hungering for anything with a flavour they demanded and received as much as 8 dollars a tin for these items. This was more than a month's pay for a man working on the road every day. By this means some of the Koreans were in possession of what to them must have been a fortune.

A few clothing items were received from the I.J.A. Boots, all very old and mainly of small sizes were issued after the guards had made their selection. 260 pairs shorts – Dutch pattern and with a waist measurement of 27″ – and a similar number of old shirts also were issued. Small as the quantity was and despite their defects, they were most welcome.

The constant rumours as to the date when the camp would close and the repeated postponement of the move had in turn heartening and depressing effects on the sick. A number of the more seriously ill cases had hung on grimly for weeks in the hope that they would be shifted any day to the south where better hospital facilities and food, particularly eggs, would be available. There is no doubt that the delay was caused by the failure of the Engineers to link the two ends of the railway, for it was learned later that a rock cutting south of Nieke had presented a greater task than at first was estimated and the north-south railway was not ready for through traffic until 20th October.

On 16th October a medical classification with the object of selecting 500 fit men was ordered. It appears that there was some intention of removing the fit men of the Force to some area where again they would be engaged on constructional works. Of the 1,500 men in camp, only 490 measured up to the fit category, 87 as fit for light duty only and the balance of over 900 as unfit for any duties. It was pointed out that if the fit men moved the sick could not be provided for and that at least 150 men would have to remain if the hospital patients were to be given a chance of survival. On 29th October a nominal roll to be completed by 5th November was called for and Camp Headquarters was informed that the move would commence soon after that date.

The position regarding essential medical supplies had become most grave since none of the requirements submitted to Lieut Tanio had been forthcoming. Strong representations were made to the I.J.A administration through Korayasu (Interpreter) who suggested that a memorandum be prepared setting out the minimum requirements and in the event of the I.J.A. Headquarters being unable to supply that the Camp Commander offer to pay for the purchase of the supplies at Rangoon or Bankok. Korayasu indicated that supplies were available at those places. The officers willingly offered to subscribe the sum of $1,500 for the purpose and this amount was mentioned in the memorandum.

The solitary result of this request was the supply of 138 yards of muslin butter cloth for which Lieut Fukuda charged $1.00 per yard.

After five months of asking, both by Force Headquarters and individual Camp Commanders two bags of rice polishings were delivered on 29th October, together with two cases of Ebos (Yeast) tablets. These were of the greatest value in the treatment of beri beri which was increasing considerably and had accounted for over 30 deaths since the beginning of the month.

The health situation during October is summarised hereunder:

	10th Oct	20th Oct	31st Oct
Cholera	–	–	–
Malaria	194	152	170
Ulcers	303	333	352
Dysentery & Diarrhoea	157	135	104
Beri Beri	180	205	167
Miscellaneous	63	74	77
Pneumonia	26	24	18
Total in hospital	923	923	888
Sick in lines	51	57	49
Total sick	974	980	937
Strength	1524	1481	1417
Deaths during period	43	43	63

Songkurai Camp (No. 2)

By 7th August, when Major Tracey and his battalion of 866 A.I.F., made up of 600 men from No. 1 camp and 266 from Nieke, had concentrated in No. 2 Camp they found conditions worse than in any other camps of the Force.

The British troops – originally 1,600 but now reduced by deaths to just under 1,000 – had suffered unmercifully. Their work task was the construction of a large bridge over the river adjacent to the camp. So severe were the demands of the Engineer Officer-in-charge, Lieut Abe, that men unfit to walk had to be carried on their comrades' backs to parade and thence to work on the bridge where they were forced to haul heavy logs and beams from a sitting position. Men had been and continued to be beaten (until the completion of the bridge on 20th August) with wire whips and bamboo sticks, and unfit men were punched and kicked, not for disciplinary reasons but with the object of driving them to make efforts beyond their strength. Lieut Abe made no attempt to stop the brutal treatment being meted out by his men.

Although officers were not forced to work on the bridge, so many were in hospital that it was impossible to organise them into works and hygiene squads as was done in the A.I.F. Camps. The proportion of sick in the camp was extremely high and the death rate was mounting. With no men available for essential camp duties sanitation had collapsed. The whole situation had got out of control and the morale of the men was extremely low.

Major Tracey reports that on his arrival "hygiene had been completely neglected, food containers were covered with flies and not washed between meals, all food was left uncovered and the floors of the kitchen were inches deep in mud and waste food. The other Ranks' huts and hospital (they were all one) beggared description. Both the inside and outside of the huts were fouled and the excreta had not been cleaned up for days.

No facilities existed for the sterilization of cooking and eating utensils, or for washing or bathing those too ill to make their way to the adjacent creek. The latrines were in close proximity to the sleeping quarters and were full to the brim, while maggots covered the surrounding earth."

Major Tracey and his party put these matters right as quickly as possible – new cookhouses were built, old latrines filled in and new ones dug, sterilization points established and a large wood supply cut and stacked. These steps immediately raised the morale of the camp from the very low ebb to which it had fallen. In spite of these improvements in hygiene it was not until the movement of the large party to Burma that the conditions in the camp could be said to be satisfactory. The daily sight of bodies being taken to the cemetery had had a most distressing effect.

Regarding rations, the scale for August was particularly bad. Rice was issued in good quantities, but the supplementary ration consisted of weevil-eaten beans and small quantities of fly-blown boxed yak. A small amount of fresh meat was issued but did little more than flavour the grass stews.

In September the position improved immeasurably – the boxed yak was of fair quality and much larger quantity, split peas replaced lima beans and sweet potatoes were issued in fair quantities. By October the boxed yak had been replaced by smaller quantities of fresh meat. Canteen stocks were available from Nieke and for some time small quantities were purchased and carried by parties in packs. Later, larger supplies became available and were delivered by elephant.

Working conditions for the early part of August were as severe as in any camp, due mainly to the urgency for the completion of the bridge over the river. For this period conditions approximated those existing in Pond's battalion and it is suggested that reference be made to the section dealing with the meaning of a "working day". During September the conditions improved and men were returning to camp at 1900 hours. In October 150 to 160 men were being supplied daily for work – many men had suffered minor injuries on quarry work owing to flying chips causing serious abrasions that developed into ulcers. On 11th November road and railway work ceased.

By the evacuation to Burma Hospital on 2nd September of 620 British and Australian personnel the strain of the administrative and medical staffs was greatly relieved. Immediately prior to the evacuation Lieut Wakabyashi of the P.O.W. administration had arrived and a considerate outlook on his part reduced the number being sent to work. The result of all these improvements was that by the middle of September the camp could be said to be in an excellent condition, while co-operation between British and Australian administrative officers and all Other Ranks was all that could be desired. After the tragedies of the recent months (for instance 268 deaths during August alone) such improvements were none too soon.

Additions to the strength of the camp were made on 24th September and 7th November when 250 and 107 Australian troops arrived from Shimo Songkurai and Taimonta respectively. Ten days after the arrival of the latter group an advanced party left for Kanburi and by the movement at short periods after that date the complete evacuation of the camp was effected.

Tanbaya Hospital, Burma

It has been reasonably assumed that the establishment of the above hospital was due to the recommendation submitted by Major Bruce Hunt, A.A.M.C. on 26th June to the effect that if the more serious of the patients were transferred to a hospital at or near a railhead they could be provided with more adequate ration and therefore would have a better chance of life.

Apparently, the Force Commander was given a sympathetic hearing when he represented Major Hunt's case for on 29th June Lieut Tanio, a Japanese medical officer attached to I.J.A. Headquarters at Nieke, accompanied by Major Phillips arrived at No. 1 Camp and informed the camp authorities that they were en route to Burma to select the site for a base hospital to which 2,000 men of the Force would be transferred.

Lieut Tanio gave instructions that men were to be medically classified at once. Those selected for transfer were to be men suffering from chronic diseases to the extent that they be unfit for work for two months and also Class II and older men. Patients suffering from infectious diseases (except chronic dysentery) and those in a dangerously ill condition were not to be included.

After all the preliminary arrangements had been made and the sick had been heartened by the thought of being given a chance to regain their health, it was most disappointing when it was announced on 9th July that the establishment of the hospital had been postponed indefinitely.

However, on 21st July it was announced that the scheme would be put into effect but that the number of patients would be 1,250 instead of 2,000 as was originally proposed. Three days later Major Hunt accompanied Col. Banno to Tanbaya – the site of the hospital – on the railway about

50 miles north-west from Lower Songkurai. Here a conference was held with Lieut Saito an I.J.A. administrative officer who informed Major Hunt that no move would take place for a week after his return on 28th July. On 30th July, however, in typical Japanese style Major Hunt and his advance party were given one hour's notice to pack and move off by road to Tanbaya. The careful orders which had been issued by Force Headquarters in consultation with I.J.A. Headquarters were discarded and the movement then became a sort of catch as catch can.

The organization of the hospital was to be as follows:

O.C. Hospital	Major B. Hunt, A.A.M.C.
Adm. Commandant	Lt-Col C.T. Hutchinson, M.C. – ex Force HQ.
Administrative personnel	3 Officers & 50 other ranks.
Medical Staff	7 Officers & 130 other ranks.

Actually, the number of patients to be moved was to become over 1,900 mainly as a result of the efforts of Lieut Wakabayashi, I.J.A. Commander of No. 2 Camp. By 7th September the following transferers had been made:

Original Camp	British	A.I.F.
Nieke	160	138
No. 1 Camp	3	320
No. 2 Camp	752	406*
No. 3 Camp	146	–

* From personnel originally at Nola and Nieke.

The 50 selected from No. 3 Camp could not be transferred on account of the cholera outbreak at that time.

Up to 29th September the deaths at Tanbaya Hospital had reached the tragic figures of 282 British troops and 64 A.I.F. Many of the British troops who had left No. 2 Camp were desperately ill on arrival and about 20 had died en route. Major Hunt reported that the chief cause of death amongst the British had been starvation, due to men whilst sick with dysentery and malaria either voluntarily or in some cases acting on medical advice having refrained from eating anything like an adequate daily ration. The A.I.F. on the whole had been better trained in this respect and the results in his opinion justified the policy of compulsorily feeding the sick.

The rations up to this date had been poor but the rice ration had been increased to about 19 ozs per man per day. Meat issue was about 1.5 ozs per day and the vegetables which comprised mainly egg-fruit had little vitamin content with the result that already there were 563 cases of beri beri. A larger supply of beans had been asked for but until the end of September only ⅓ bag had been issued daily. A number of cases of acute cardiac beri beri occurred usually amongst men debilitated from other diseases.

In addition, there were 512 cases of dysentery, many of them amoebic in type, but hygiene control had assisted materially in stopping the spread of this disease in the camp. There were 346 cases of malaria, largely of the MT type of a very virulent nature and 219 malaria convalescents. Ulcer cases numbered 332, many of such a serious nature that amputations became essential if the lives of the men were to be saved.

Sickness amongst the medical staff also was presenting great difficulties. Only about 60 of the 157 personnel were fit for duty, 38 were anticipated to be ill for at least six weeks and the balance for a longer period. Major Hunt asked for an additional Australian medical officer and approval was given by Commander A.I.F. troops for Capt Hendry to go forward from No. 2 Camp.

By 10th October the number of deaths had risen to 329 British and 88 Australian, representing 31.3% and 10.1% of the arrivals respectively. Beri Beri cases had increased to 600 and many ulcer cases had reached an appalling state. It was estimated that if the hospital had to be moved at this stage arrangements would have to be made for at least 800 stretcher cases of whom 50% could be expected to die.

It was agreed, in the circumstances, that if evacuation commenced about the middle of October as was anticipated at this juncture only the fittest of men should undertake the journey south, the remainder to be kept at Tanbaya until they had recovered sufficiently to make the journey with a fair degree of certainty of reaching Kanburi alive.

The bean ration, considered by Major Hunt to be so important in beri beri cases had increased to a bag a day. A visit to a nearby "A" Force

Camp elicited the information that with a similar number of men to feed 3 to 4 bags were being issued daily. This was pointed out to the I.J.A. administrative officer and although for weeks the Camp Commander had been told that an increased ration was impossible the bean ration then went up to 3 bags a day. Of the 600 beri beri cases 400 had contracted the disease in Tanbaya.

The additional beans combined with a daily issue of 3 ozs rice polishings began to have a striking effect but only after 100 men had died of beri beri.

By the first week in November the water supply had become a problem. The cookhouse had been shifted twice as neighbouring streams had dried up and now a 750-yard carry was necessary.

The number of deaths continued to rise, and by 10th November 438 British troops had died out of 1061 arrivals and 161 Australians from 871 arrivals.

In view of the prevalent talk of possible movement about this time it was deemed expedient to carry out a medical examination which revealed that only 4 Officers and 53 Other Ranks were fit to march, 66 Officers and 955 Other Ranks were fit to travel sitting and 2 Officers and 139 Other Ranks fit to travel lying. In addition over 100 were considered too ill to travel.

By the time the evacuation of the hospital commenced on 21st November the position had deteriorated still further and the number unfit to travel had risen to over 300.

Up to 24th November the admissions and deaths at Tanbaya Hospital were as under:

	British			Australian		
Camp of origin	Arrivals	Deaths	Percentage	Arrivals	Deaths	Percentage
Nieke	159	69	43.4%	138	27	19.6%
No. 1 Camp	3	1	33.3%	320	71	22.2%
No. 2 Camp	752	341	44.0%	406	83	20.4%
No. 5 Camp	147	69	47.0%	-	-	-
	1061	480	45.2%	864	181	21.0%

The evacuation to Kanburi commenced on 21st November and the personnel left in Burma by the end of November were as follows:

British Patients	185 }	of these the expected mortality was nearly
Australian Patients	135 } 100	
Medical staff	55	
Camp Duties		

Pond's Battalion – August–November

August opened with very little alteration in the conditions – cholera still was increasing, the ration position was stationary, the weather still heavy rain and working hours still inhuman. The only matter to be placed on the credit side was the receipt of the first pay for 3½ months.

Working pay for the men was 20 cents per day (coolies incidentally were receiving over one dollar for the same work), and after deductions from officers' pay and contributions from the men it was possible to allow 2½ cents per man per day for the sick. Still more welcome was the appearance of river barges with canteen supplies and during the month these supplies included tinned fish, eggs, gula malacca, bananas, biscuits, tinned milk, pomeloes, and peanut toffee.

Prices usually made the purchase of these items except in very small quantities out of the question, but by the sale of watches and other valuables to the Japanese guards and, unfortunately the sale of clothes to the Thais many lives undoubtedly were saved by the benefit obtained from these foods. An appreciation must be expressed for the splendid donation of $248.00 to the Amenities Fund made by the British troops in the vicinity.

In spite of spirited protests by Capts Barnett (Adjutant) and Mills (Medical Officer) to Lieut Murayama against the starvation of the sick no improvement was forthcoming. So empathic was Capt Mills on one occasion that it called forth a challenge by Murayama to a fight to the death (with Japanese weapons) to show, as he said, how superior were the Japanese to the English. Capt Mills counter-offered to fight with fists but this was not accepted. On a subsequent occasion at Taimonta Capt Mills through a misunderstanding over the sending of men to work was compelled to kneel for a long period before Murayama's sergeant and receive repeated blows on the head with a bamboo stick. During this period the striking and face slapping of the men was frequent but seldom very severe. Four officers in addition to the two mentioned above received "bashings", Capts Lloyd, Gahan and Curlewis for endeavouring to intervene on behalf of the men and Capt Kemp for arguing concerning rations.

By 10th August the only matter for comment had been a sharp rise in dysentery and diarrhoea, to be followed by an equally sharp fall.

On 13th August the peak of the cholera epidemic was reached, 135 patients being isolated. From that date there was a steady decline and by the end of the month only 48 were quarantined. The despatch on 16th August of another batch of 80 of the very sick to Kanburi Hospital again greatly relieved the strain on the medical staff and vastly improved the position as regards accommodation.

Continual carrying and soaking of the tentage had resulted in almost all tents rotting and tearing. The natural consequence of this was the restriction of space, necessitating all men, whatever their malady, sleeping so close together as to be touching one another. Obviously this was not conductive to reducing the sickness figures.

As mentioned previously, it was at this period that it became apparent that frantic efforts were being made to finish the section of the railway according to schedule, and for the first time gelignite was introduced to replace the antiquated method of removing tons of rock by means of the pick. Although the Japanese Engineers' ideas of blasting were primitive in the extreme, there is no doubt that the strain on the men thereby was greatly lessened. Hours of work, however, increased and varied from 13 to 18 hours a day.

It was during this period that officers, men and coolies were herded together working literally shoulder to shoulder. The ten-minute rests for smoking were abolished in the mornings and apart from lunch the rest periods did not commence until 1700 hours.

Rations over the ten days showed rice plentiful; meat, although made available in one large and two small issues, averaged 3 ozs per man per day; four gallons of oil and four gallons of curry were issued for 300 odd men; and one issue each of 3 ozs dried vegetables and 5 ozs dried fish also were received. Protests against this totally inadequate diet still were of no avail.

For the last period of the month there was little variation. On 25th August the return of 34 men who had been left at Tamarumpat as too ill to travel brought the camp total strength up to 429 of whom 209 were sick and not fit for work of any kind. Conditions in the small camp at Tamarumpat had been particularly trying as no fit man had been left for camp duties. All medical work was attended to by Sgt Boan, R.A.P. Sgt, 2/29 Bn, and he deserves the greatest credit for the responsible work he performed at this time. During the two months 14 of the party died.

On 31st August the third and final party of sick was evacuated to Kanburi. Although of incalculable benefit to the sick themselves the evacuation did not relieve the position for the remainder as much as was to be hoped. The sick were still receiving only two meals a day of rice gruel as they were not assisting in the construction of the railway; for the whole of the month the shortage of wood in close proximity to the camp had necessitated weary men returning from work collecting logs over the last ½ mile and carrying them back to camp for use as fuel in the kitchen; the wearing out of much used bandages resulted in old shirts and banana leaves being substituted for the dressings on ulcers; the continual flooding of latrines and a rise of 30 feet in the river caused grave concern as the available space for fresh latrines was exhausted.

It is of interest to note that at this time several men whose nerves were not equal to the crossing of the narrow logs on the high level bridge when returning from work at night preferred to swim 80 yards in pitch darkness across a fast flowing river down which logs and trees were floating. Two strong protests were submitted by Lt-Col Pond to Lt-Col Banno during this month. Copies will be found in Appendices IV and V.

News that the camp again would be moved in a few days' time relieved the tension and for once the projected move took place on the day appointed.

On 3rd September the party again was put on the road to march, and in three days under appalling conditions covered 33 miles, retracing their steps north for the second time. After the evacuation of the sick south there still were 347 in camp but inspection of these disclosed that recuperating cholera cases were unfit to move, and 60 of these were left under an officer with a Japanese guard. They remained in this camp until they moved by barge to Kanburi Hospital on 30th October. As no work was allotted to this party beyond camp duties, rations improved considerably under Korean guards no longer supervised by Murayama and canteen supplies were plentiful, this party experienced the best conditions for two months of any personnel in Thailand.

The marching party after these deductions now only numbered 287 of the original 700, deaths having amounted to 71. The monsoonal rains had ceased but were replaced by intense and stifling heat. Again, the two night halts were in disused cooly lines, totally inadequate tattered and torn tentage being the only cover, and excreta and vomitus abounding. On arrival at Taimonta at nightfall a most distressing looking camp awaited the troops – hut accommodation was at a premium and space could be made available only by moving coolies and crowding them to one end of the hut.

Again, the cooly [sic] filth was everywhere and on this occasion body lice made themselves felt in a serious manner (it was not until some months after the return of the Force to Changi that this pest could be brought under control). The rains had recommenced and left the huts in a sea of black slippery mud. The only latrine was one 20 feet from the hut which had to be shared with the coolies. Within two days this trench was crawling with maggots, was foul smelling and water-logged. Rations had to be served and eaten within a few yards of it. For three weeks rations were supplied by the I.J.A. from the same kitchen as the coolies and consisted of rice, a fish-flavoured soup and chillies.

The effect of these conditions was immediately apparent in that there was a rise in the sickness rate. Skin complaints, dysentery and malaria soared and of the 287 men only slightly over half were fit for work which had commenced in spite of the arduous journey on the morning after arrival. A further protest was forwarded to Col Banno on 10th September.

Within a fortnight even Lieut Murayama realised that unless an alteration was made there would be no men available for work. To cure this he selected a new camp site and all sick men were turned out to work with coolies clearing the land and erecting bamboo huts.

From that date and for the ensuing seven weeks the camp site occupied was the best for the whole period. Admittedly the attap roofs leaked, water had to be drawn from a stream 300 yards away and sandflies were particularly bad, but the benefit of being in a camp that had not been occupied by coolies and actually was out of sight of coolies was very great.

The work in September and the first half of October varied considerably; several late nights would occur (even up to 0230 hours) and then a series of early nights when work finished at 2030 hours would be experienced.

On 15th October the rail laying party from the north passed the camp and men were taken off working in the cuttings and put to breaking stones in a quarry to provide ballast for the line. The food problem was as bad as at any time previously. For three weeks the diet was rice, a square inch of dried fish once a day and a very little towgay mixed with leaves plucked from the jungle. From information furnished by Korean guards it is certain that Murayama was not distributing rations issued to him for the prisoners of war.

For the last ten days of October a new form of torture was instituted. A party of 100 men was called for each day to carry Japanese railway gear from Nieke to Taimonta or from Taimonta to Koncoita. In both cases the return journey amounted to 15 miles.

The route was along the line and meant the men walking on the irregularly placed sleepers or on the hard gravel at the sides; the lightest load would be a bundle of 5 picks, the heaviest an anvil, and on both journeys empty train after empty train would pass the struggling men without any effort being made to relieve them.

Without doubt these journeys were the culminating point in cruelty to the sick. Staggering under their heavy loads, riddled with malaria, with ulcered and cut feet, men collapsed over and over again and their loads had to be redistributed to other already overburdened men. On one occasion a Warrant Officer, a particularly strong P.T. Instructor previously in the British Regular Forces, had to drag himself the last three kilometres back to camp on hands and knees.

The beginning of November at last brought rest for the men. The original party of 700 now reduced to 289, could at a pinch produce 80 men for a working party, and on 6th November all men were put to their final test. Orders were received that the whole camp would move north to Nieke carrying all the sick – about 50 – including 26 stretcher cases. This meant that if 8 men were allocated to a stretcher they would have to include sick men to carry their own gear, the sick man's gear and also take a handle on the stretcher. This march will remain indelibly seared in many men's minds. Stretchers under normal conditions became heavy after even a half mile carry.

The carrying of these improvised stretchers, ladened with a very sick patient and his gear, by sick men burdened with their own gear along railway sleepers or rough and uneven ground at the side throughout the hottest hours of a Thailand sun, brought about the collapse and subsequent serious illness of many men who, till then, had borne the brunt of heavy work. Most stretcher parties found that 100 yards was the limit of endurance before the patient had to be lowered and a rest taken.

The first party covered the journey in seven hours but were told on arrival that accommodation was short and that 100 odd men would have to proceed another 9 miles to Songkurai. On arrival of Lt-Col Pond he ordered that Capt Curlewis call for volunteers and take them the remaining distance. The state of the men was so bad on arrival that the volunteers were insufficient and others as they fell exhausted had to be conscripted and told that they would have to march further. The party got away at 2100 hours and covered the journey in 6 hours and were finally settled in their new huts at 0430 hours.

The following morning these 107 men were absorbed into Major Tracey's party and became part and parcel of that camp until the return journey to Kanburi was commenced. Of the party remaining at Nieke little remains to be said. The accommodation as usual was totally inadequate, a hut being shared with Dutch Ps.O.W. Lice and vermin of all kinds were abundant and practically all men were suffering from scabies. 40 men were employed in an I.J.A. Ration Store while the remainder were engaged on camp duties. On 21st November the party under Lt-Col Pond commenced the move back to Kanburi by train.

It is known that at least 153 personnel of Pond's battalion died during the period May-December, 83 in the camps occupied by the various detachments and a further 70 after evacuation to Wanyai and Kanburi. The causes of the 83 deaths in camp included the following: Cholera 44; Typhus 4; Pneumonia 3; Jaundice 1.

The balance of 31 died from malnutrition, malaria and chronic dysentery, aggravated in each case by the long hours of work and exposure. The average strength of Pond's battalion during the months of May-October was 530.

Chapter 8

Conditions during November and Return of the Force to Singapore

The following is a description of the conditions encountered during November, and then the return of the Force to Singapore.

Upper Songkurai Camp

With the move south to Kanburi now imminent, the spirits of all ranks rose considerably particularly in this camp where the average death rate was 6.5 per day and no diminution in the number of sick was forthcoming. Knowing that the I.J.A. had failed to fulfil any of their many previous promises there lurked in everyone's mind the thought that the move for any man individually might come too late. There was another cholera scare and so far all the natives had not been vaccinated.

200 men were still being sent out to work in the quarry and on the railway and even this comparatively small number was difficult to provide. Fit men, however, were preferring to go to work rather than stay in camp in a depressing and unhealthy atmosphere. Work continued until the 15th of the month and by this date the camp strength had fallen from 1,732 to 1,318, comprising 454 British troops and 864 Australians, of whom 404 of the former and 711 of the latter were still in hospital.

Some 250 men were transferred to a group of new huts about ½ mile from the main camp. These huts had been completed for weeks except for the attap roofing. As soon as this transfer was made, cooly [sic] gangs entered the camp and commenced to demolish a portion of the old camp thereby nullifying any benefits arising from the action already referred to in the direction of reducing overcrowding. In view of the impending move the resultant disorganisation and interference to the sick could have been avoided. But this had been the answer to all the protests lodged about accommodation for months past.

On 6th November some surgical dressings and medical supplies came to hand. While "better late than never", the supply was quite inadequate and comprised Creosote pills, quinine, a small quantity of sulphur but sufficient to start treatment of scabies which were now universal, and infinitesimal quantities of Emetine and Vitamin B1 ampoules. The Emetine was only sufficient to treat three dysentery cases for three days and the ampoules sufficient for two cases of beri beri. From the manner in which they were issued, one would have thought that all our requests for medical stores had been fully and promptly met. In no case was this the fact.

Rations had improved out of all recognition and canteen supplies in small quantities were being brought in by personnel from No. 2 Camp. Mention already has been made of the receipt of rice polishings and yeast tablets at this time.

It almost appeared that with the transfer of Lieut Fukuda to Nieke and his replacement by a Probationary Officer that the stumbling block to the dozens of requests for better treatment made from time to time had been removed. In any case relations with the I.J.A. now were better than ever previously and there were many examples of a genuine desire to alleviate the conditions of the sick and to improve the rations.

Every day conflicting orders were given as to the move and finality was not reached until 16th November when 500 of the fittest men were instructed to stand by in readiness to move the following day. At 1900 hours that day this party was assembled alongside the railway line ready to entrain but only two trucks arrived and a party of 50, including Lt-Col Kappe, departed at about 2100 hours. The balance of 450 returned to camp for the night, stood by all the next day and on the 19th marched to Nieke to entrain there. As a result of the necessity to leave behind in the camp 150 fit men to care for the sick many men not fit to undertake this march of 11 kilometres without adversely affecting their health had perforce to be included in the party.

On 24th November the I.J.A. administration issued orders that on the following day 400 hospital patients accompanied by the camp maintenance group of 150 were to march to Songkurai en route to Nieke. This was a perfectly absurd order which the I.J.A. Camp Commander must have been well aware was incapable of being carried out.

It had been pointed out by Lt-Col Kappe some weeks previously when the proposition of moving the whole camp personnel to No. 2 Camp was first mooted that with 150 to 160 stretcher patients to be shifted at least 4 days would be needed to complete evacuation.

Major Johnston, who had been left in charge of the sick, protested that the scheme was fantastic, particularly now that it was required that the move should take place in one day. After much argument the Engineers gave in and agreed that the remnants of the camp should be entrained from outside the camp on 26th November.

The entrainment of the sick was a scene of great confusion. Every detail for the move had been carefully worked out and lying, sitting and standing cases with a proportion of fit men and medical orderlies had been allocated to trucks so that the maximum of attention could be given and discomfort reduced to a minimum. All this was to go by the board, however, and the sick, regardless of their category, were literally rushed on to the trains by the I.J.A.

Eventually only a small rear party of 22 in charge of Lieut Tweedie remained to close the camp and care for 5 men who were dying. As the time approached for the departure of this party one man was so low that it was obviously only a matter of an hour or less before he died. Becoming impatient because Lieut Tweedie demanded that this man be allowed to die in peace the I.J.A. sergeant suggested to this officer that the death of the man be hastened by action on Tweedie's part. Needless to say, he refused.

Songkurai Camp

Here the improved conditions brought about by the new Camp administration under Lieut Wakabayashi and Lt-Col Dillon continued up to the time of departure for the south.

Similar confusion to that which occurred at No. 3 Camp was to arise when movement actually commenced. Parties were drawn up in pouring rain and made to stand by for hours, then only to be informed that trains would not pick up except at Nieke. The evacuation, however, was comparatively simple as No. 2 Camp had very few sick on their hands at this stage. Despite this, there were at least 200 men who were not really fit enough to undertake the 7½ mile march over railway sleepers carrying their own packs.

Train Journey to Kanburi

No time was allowed for organisation of any sort at Nieke. As parties arrived they were hurried on to the first empty trucks that became available. Where possible a meal was provided by a small party under Capt Barnett, 8 Aust Div Signals, who continued to do sterling work.

The absence of organisation for the journey to Kanburi was in keeping with the state of affairs with which the Force had had to contend during the previous six months.

The journey south was uncomfortable in the extreme but the relief of the men to feel that at long last they were moving away from the scenes of so many months cruelty caused them to make light of their discomforts.

Open trucks packed to capacity, derailments, delays of hours in the blazing tropical sun, hurried transfers from one train to another sometimes in the middle of the night and in the rain all were endured cheerfully. Yet these factors combined with lack of sufficient drinking water and periods of between 13 and 24 hours between meals all contributed to bringing on illnesses among the weaker men, 46 of whom died during the course of the journey.

Kanburi

The first party of the Force to arrive at Kanburi was the 50 men from No. 3 Camp. It was hoped that this party would have been used as an advanced party to make arrangements for the reception of the following train groups, but owing to the fact that a small group of "H" Force were still at Kanburi this party was quartered in an adjoining camp. With a little foresight on the part of the I.J.A. tents could have been erected, additional kitchens made ready and latrines dug prior to the arrival of the larger of the larger bodies. In fact, however, Lt-Col Kappe's party was not transferred to the main camp until after the first trains had marched in.

The task of Lieut-Col Dillon, who had been placed in command of the camp, was no sinecure. For days train parties were marched into the camp at all hours of the day or night, there was always a shortage of tents to cover the men and the kitchen and latrine accommodation on account of the shortage of tools was hardly sufficient until parties started to move back to Malaya.

Water supplies were inadequate and the men had to walk a mile to the river to wash. The food issued by the I.J.A. was very poor. Had it not been for the fact that the purchase of eggs, dried fish and fruit in quantity now was possible, the starvation suffered in the north would have been continued.

By the time the concentration was completed, 1,000 men had been admitted to the hospital established two months earlier by "H" Force. Although the accommodation was little better than in the up-country camps, the sick were to enjoy the advantages of extra diet provided from funds contributed by the officers and the absence of the worry of being ordered out on working parties before their recovery had been effected. Despite these better conditions 186 of the Force (details of A.I.F. not known) died at this hospital within the first three weeks.

When it was decided to clear the main body of the Force from Kanburi Capt Barnett was selected by the I.J.A. to remain in command of the sick. Unfortunately, among the A.I.F. patients in the hospital was Major B. Hunt who had developed acute cardiac beri beri. A considerable sum contributed from officers' pay was left with the Senior Medical Officer, Lt-Col Huston, for the purchase of extra food for the very ill.

Lieut Wakabayashi, who it will be remembered adopted a humane attitude to the sick in No. 2 Camp, was left as the I.J.A. Supervising Officer and it was felt that he would at least not obstruct any action taken to restore the men to normal health.

Return to Malaya

Soon after arrival at Kanburi it was announced that the first to move on would be 1,000 fit men – two parties of 500 each – who would be required to work on arrival at their destination – Sumatra, Japan and Singapore were all mentioned as possibilities.

To obtain 1,000 fit men was a sheer impossibility and when the first party of 500 A.I.F. was formed it was necessary to include several light sick. The second party originally comprised 380 A.I.F. and 120 British troops but sickness of the latter demanded an increase in the number of Australians. The Commander, A.I.F. Troops decided to adhere to his policy of accompanying the fit men.

The first party left by train on 2nd December and next day arrived at Bangkok Docks and learned that the next stage was to be by sea. The troops remained at Bangkok for a week, quartered in a dock goods shed. Food here could have been considered reasonable had not the I.J.A. Quartermaster (Toyama) appropriated one-third of the total rations for the 20 or 30 members of the guard. Lieut Iwamota arranged occasional purchases from the Thais and made efforts to obtain larger and better rations and went to some personal trouble to obtain medical supplies. After everything had been arranged for the latter, it was discovered that the I.J.A. medical store was closed, a holiday being observed in commemoration of the opening of the Malayan campaign.

On 10th December the party embarked as deck cargo on a 4000-ton steamer, arriving at Singapore on 14th December. Cover from weather on deck was inadequate but the party were not greatly inconvenienced. The food was good and the crew did all in their power to make conditions comfortable, courtesy to the Commander and his Headquarters being outstanding – a vastly different attitude to that displayed by the I.J.A.

When rain set in permission was given by the Captain for all malaria cases and other sick to be transferred to an upper hold. Before permission was granted the Captain had to be assured that there were no British troops in the party, emphatically stating that had there been any but Australians the privilege of getting under cover would not have been granted. It was apparent that the action of the Commonwealth Government in granting a naval funeral to the crews of the submarines which attacked Sydney Harbour had created a deep impression on the minds of the Captain and his officers. This incident is recorded to indicate once more the attempts made to discriminate between A.I.F. and English troops.

On 10th December the party arrived at Changi and was followed by other groups on successive days until 23rd December. One small party was diverted to Sime Road Singapore with "H" Force. With the exception of No. 1 Party, the parties had travelled from Thailand by train under conditions practically identical to those which operated on the forward journey to Thailand.

With the return to the familiar surroundings of Changi and the many happy re-unions which took place, the spirits of the men rose remarkably although their physical condition was very poor. Bad as it was many of the men with the aid of eggs etc. obtained during the week spent at Kanburi had been able to put on up to a stone in weight since leaving the Thailand Working Camps.

At the conclusion of the move back to Singapore in December the disposition of the A.I.F. Component of "F" Force was as follows:

Strength of A.I.F. Component	3,662
Deaths up country	892
Missing up country	13
Remained up country	534
Returned to Singapore	2,223
Deaths since return to Singapore	32

As a result of the return to Singapore at the end of April of the balance of the A.I.F. Component it is possible to include in this report the following information concerning the personnel left up country in December:

Strength	534
Deaths	122
Returned to Singapore	411
Location unknown	1

It is gratifying to be able to record that as a result of the rest and improved food available to them during the last five months the majority of the personnel who recently returned to Singapore are considerably restored in health and in fact appear to be more fit than the supposedly fit men who returned in December last. The Tanbaya Hospital, Burma was finally evacuated on 20th December when the personnel who had been left there moved south to Kanburi, where they remained until the recent move back to Singapore of all personnel remaining in Thailand.

It will be seen therefore that of the original 3,662 A.I.F. personnel who departed from Singapore as members of "F" Force just twelve months ago, a total of 1,060 have failed to return representing approximately 29% of the A.I.F. Component.

When the 2,025 British deaths which occurred during the same period are added it will be seen that the total fatal casualties on "F" Force as a whole amounted to 3,085 out of 6,999 or 44% of the Force.

Chapter 9

General

This report, while primarily dealing with the A.I.F. would be incomplete were reference not made to the conditions surrounding the employment of native workmen by the I.J.A.

Treatment of Natives

Information is not available as to the numbers utilised on railway construction but an estimate of 150,000 would not be excessive when Chinese, Malays and Tamils who preceded "F" Force and continued to arrive up to October are taken into consideration. Whether some of the labour was impressed also is not known but from conversations with many Chinese at work there is no doubt that attractive inducements had been held out to them to leave their homes all over Malaya and proceed north. Their rates of pay varied from $1.00 to $1.50 per day but from this sum they were compelled to make contributions towards their maintenance.

If possible, their treatment on the march through Thailand was worse than that meted out to Prisoners of War. Provision for medical attention seemed non-existent and it was not until June that English and Australian medical officers and attendants were sent from Singapore to attend to the ravages of disease amongst their ranks. Figures of their death rate are not available but observation indicates that this must have been appalling. Dead or dying coolies along the side of the road were a daily sight. In camps where cholera broke out, bodies were taken away in tins for cremation or burial.

While it is true that the outbreak of cholera amongst the Prisoners of War can be directly attributed to the total absence of any hygiene arrangements amongst the native workers, the whole blame cannot be thrust on them. It was obvious that they had no innate sense of hygiene themselves and absolutely nothing was done to teach them even the simplest rules of sanitation.

It is interesting to note that officers and men who worked shoulder to shoulder with the natives ascertained by means of surreptitious conversation that they had much in common and that universally the natives hated the I.J.A.

Pay

It was not until the end of July that the men received their first pay since leaving Changi. The majority had been able to provide themselves with a few dollars by the sale of clothing, watches and other articles to the Thais at Banpong and on the march to Nieke but these resources were quickly expended on the purchase of foodstuffs to supplement the totally inadequate rations provided by the I.J.A. From August onwards pay was received about once a month, the rates of pay in the majority of camps being as follows:

Rank	Outside work and Cooks	Permanent Camp Duty	Original Red Cross Certificate Holders
W.Os.	40 cents per day	25 cents per day	$2.30 per day
N.C.Os.	30 cents per day	15 cents per day	$2.30 per day
Ptes	25 cents per day	10 cents per day	90 cents per day

Apart from those employed on the road and railway the only personnel who received any pay were those engaged on the very limited number of camp duties recognised by the I.J.A., such as hospital staff, hygiene and cooks. There were many other tasks essential to the maintenance of the camp such as fuel collection, which involved bringing in supplies of bamboo and logs at times from more than half a mile from the camp, cremation, water parties, unloading of ration trucks etc., but despite repeated requests the I.J.A. administration refused to make any payment to the personnel employed on these tasks.

As far as was possible these personnel were paid from Camp Funds, derived from deductions from officers' and Red Cross Certificate Holders' pay and contributions from Other Ranks in receipt of pay, and a small payment also was made from the same source to hospital patients to enable them to purchase a little tobacco when such was available. No payment whatsoever was forthcoming for the period of over three weeks covered by the train journey from Singapore and the march from Banpong and when representations were made on this point to I.J.A. Headquarters it was stated that the matter again should be raised when the Force returned to Singapore.

Officers' Pay generally was at the rate of $45.00 per month for Captains and above and $32.00 per month for Lieutenants. The total amount received from the I.J.A. on account of AIF Officers' Pay for the eight months April–November was $41,760, of which $13,767 was deducted as contributions towards hospitals and supplementary rations. These contributions were disposed of in the following manner:

Tanbaya Hospital, Burma	$5,040.00
Kanburi Hospital, Thailand	$2,010.00
Local Camp Hospitals	$6,717.00
Total	$13,767.00

It is pointed out that although considerable funds were in hand for disposal comparatively little could be done to assist the sick personnel in the various camps owing to the fact that it was impracticable to obtain supplies in the majority of camps, while in those camps where canteen supplies did become available they were in relatively small quantities and at irregular intervals.

Records and Returns

Throughout the existence of the Force, most careful records were kept. In all camps diaries of events supported by strength returns, medical statistics and details of ration supplies were maintained and are available, extracts only from these having been incorporated in this report.

A general medical report already has been submitted by the Senior Medical Officer (Major Stevens) and it is anticipated that this will be enlarged upon by Major Bruce Hunt at a later date, particularly in respect of his experiences at Tanbaya Hospital and at Kanburi Hospital during the period December–April.

The returns demanded from time to time by the I.J.A. were numerous and as only the barest minimum of paper was supplied recourse was had to the use of bamboo slats for the maintenance of the detailed records from which these returns were compiled. The number and variety of these returns, listed below, tend to give the impression that the I.J.A. authorities were really solicitous for the welfare of the Force but enough has been written to show that the majority of the returns amounted to so much "red tape".

The following returns were required to be submitted in each camp and were transmitted periodically to I.J.A. Headquarters at Nieke:

1. Death certificate, signed by S.M.O. in each individual case.
2. Deaths by diseases – daily and every 10, 15 and 30 days.
3. Nominal roll of deaths – every 15 and 30 days.
4. Sickness by diseases – daily and every 10, 15 and 30 days.
5. Strength return – daily and every 10, 15 and 30 days.
6. Pay return – daily and every 10, 15 and 30 days.

It is significant to note that in the compilation of the consolidated monthly death return for I.J.A. Headquarters dysentery as the cause of death was ordered to be changed to diarrhoea. Apparently the former was a disease notifiable to higher authorities and for some sinister reason the number of deaths from dysentery was to be concealed.

Medical

Reference already has been made in the body of this report to the parlous state of the men's health upon their arrival at their destination and to the steady deterioration which followed as a direct consequence of their being put immediately to arduous and in most cases unaccustomed labour without any opportunity of recuperation from the effects of the train journey and the 100 mile march.

It was evident from the very outset that the medical staff were confronted with a situation of the gravest magnitude and that all their experience and skill would need to be applied if a major disaster were to be averted. But the worst was still to be experienced. Cholera, that most dreaded of all diseases, perpetually casting its grim shadow over the heads of the men and relentlessly taking its heavy toll of human life; malnutrition and starvation; dysentery; malaria and jungle fever; tropical ulcers developing to gangrene and necessitating amputations; in short, a situation which it is not an exaggeration to describe as equalling in its severity and gravity some of the major disasters of the world has known in recent times.

To meet all of which, what did the I.J.A. do? It failed to supply anything approaching an adequate food ration; it failed to supply other than the merest modicum of medical requirements; it failed to maintain hygienic living conditions; in short, it failed to do anything of a material nature to meet a disaster of the first magnitude – a disaster of its own making.

It has been stated elsewhere in this report, but it is a fact which will well stand repetition, that had it not been for the amazing skill and unrelenting devotion to the highest traditions of the medical profession displayed right through and without exception by the medical officers of the Force, and the tireless and in many instances courageous assistance given them by medical orderlies and others, the calamity of "F" Force would have been a far, far greater one than it was. The debt which every survivor of the Force owes to these men is appreciated by them to the full, and it is desired here and on their behalf, officially to acknowledge that debt and express their everlasting gratitude for and admiration of their work during those trying months spent in Thailand.

A full word picture of the difficulties with which the medical officers had to contend at all times in carrying out their work is impracticable in this report, but as an example it is proposed to instance the incomparable conditions under which amputations were performed in one particular camp. The operation "theatre" comprised a bamboo-slat table under a bamboo and attap awning erected in the camp area outside the hospital ward.

Instruments were sterilized as well as possible in a dixie of water boiled over a nearby open fire, the patient was brought to the theatre, the anaesthetic administered and there, in the open air, without any protection from the dust and filth which abounded, without any of the accoutrements normally available to the operating surgeon, such as artificial lighting, mask, gloves etc. a major operation was performed. The patient then was returned to his "bed" in the ward – a ground sheet and maybe a blanket spread over a few square feet of space on a bamboo staging in a dirty and dilapidated bamboo hut, there to continue his battle for life alongside his sick comrades.

The truly amazing fact which emerges is that some at least of the amputation cases have won that grim battle, surely a remarkable testimony to their grit and determination to win through, and to the care and skill of the doctors who performed the operations.

It is apparent that much valuable information and experience has been gained by the medical officers of the Force as a result of the activities in Thailand, particularly arising from the experimentation and improvisation which circumstances necessitated. These technical matters are outside the scope and function of this report but have been fully covered in separate reports submitted by the medical officers concerned to the ADMS AIF Malaya. No doubt these medical reports in due course will be made available to the medical profession in order that the lessons learned may be studied and applied for the benefit of humanity generally.

Cemeteries

Cemeteries were established in all AIF Camps and such maintenance and improvement work as was practicable with the limited resources of labour tools and material available was carried out from time to time. The bulk of the work associated with the cemeteries was performed by Chaplains Polain (2/26 Bn) and Walsh (2/30 Bn).

In accordance with IJA orders all bodies were cremated. Portion of the ashes was collected, placed in small bamboo containers and interned, the burial service being read by the Chaplain, or by the Camp Commander when no Chaplain was available. A record of the individual graves was maintained.

In the two main AIF Camps Nos 1 and 3, memorial crosses were erected and although it is anticipated that the jungle will overgrow the graves it should be possible by these means to locate the cemeteries for some time to come. The cemetery at Lower Taimonta has been desecrated by the railway running through the site.

Church Services

In every camp the difficulties experienced in conducting religious services were enormous. Five Chaplains, two of whom died and one of whom was evacuated to Kanburi on account of illness, accompanied the Force from

Singapore. This number was insufficient to serve all camps as they were situated, but even at the camps where they were stationed the finding of the congregation was the main problem. The working men left camp too early and returned too late for services and the majority of the hospital patients were too ill to be moved, but in spite of these obstacles the Chaplains utilised every opportunity of furthering the spiritual welfare of the men.

In addition to carrying out their normal duties when practicable, the Chaplains rendered valuable assistance in many other directions, ranging from maintenance work in the cemeteries to performing mess orderly duties.

Entertainments

There is little to comment upon under this heading. Until the railway was completed neither performance nor time was available for its indulgence. The promises held out prior to leaving Changi of bands and gramophones was not fulfilled. Such instruments as had been brought away had had to be left at Banpong at the commencement of the march.

Requests to be permitted to provide even the simplest form of entertainment for the troops were met with point blank refusals by the I.J.A. In Pond's battalion on one occasion a quartet which had returned from work at 2100 hours attempted to cheer the hospital patients with a few songs. They were immediately sent for by Lieut Murayama, lined up and struck severely three times on the face with closed fist.

In spite of the general ban on attempts to break the monotony of the evenings nearly all camps organized "after dark" lectures and talks on all manner of subjects and a few camp concerts were held towards the end. Reading was practically impossible for the reason that almost all the books that had been brought from Changi either had been ruined by rain during the march or had been used in desperation by the men as cigarette paper, no other being procurable.

After the completion of the railway and when the troops had returned to Kanburi the restrictions were lifted and Captain Booth (2/30 Bn) organised open air concerts with the assistance of a broken-down piano and a few instruments brought out from Banpong. These concerts were the first real entertainment the men had enjoyed for seven long months and needless to say they were greatly appreciated.

Morale

Frequent references have been made in the course of this report to the high morale of the AIF troops throughout the eight months spent in Thailand. No more need to be said on this matter other than to repeat that whilst the grim and trying circumstances under which they found themselves forced to live inevitably found out weaknesses in the characters of some of the men, on the other hand that same set of adverse circumstances seemed to bring out the very best in others, and it can be said that the standard of morale and the behaviour of the larger proportion of the AIF personnel left little to be desired.

The position in this respect may best be summarized by quoting the following letter addressed to Lt-Col Kappe by Lt-Col Harris Commander of the Force, upon his return to Changi:

> On the eve of the dissolution of "F" Force I am writing to convey to you my deep appreciation of the loyal manner in which you and all ranks of the AIF of "F" Force under your command backed me up in the grisly times that we have endured together. There was no call, however arduous, that I have made on the officers and men of the AIF that they did not respond to wholeheartedly, and the way in which they helped their sick 'cobbers' and British comrades through long months of misery is beyond praise.
>
> At all times they met the most desperate situations with a clear courage and unswerving devotion to duty. I fought as a subaltern alongside the AIF at Pozieres in 1916, and their gallantry during that battle is imprinted indelibly on my memory. The ordeal your men were called upon to endure in Thailand was, if possible, a higher test of courage and endurance as it took place, not in the heat of battle, but in the depths of the jungle when all hope of survival seemed lost. They were challenged by circumstances of almost unbelievable horror, and they did not draw back from the challenge.
>
> We have left many of the best of our Force in Thailand jungles but I assure you that the part played by the AIF will be reported by me personally to the War Cabinet – Through Sir Edward Grigg – on my return to England.
>
> We are all sorry that the Force is breaking up, but I know that the firm comradeship cemented by the dangers and disasters we have endured together will be a lasting one.
>
> *(Signed) Stanley Harris*

Citations and Commendations

The Commander of the AIF Component of "F" Force wishes to place on record his appreciation of the excellent services performed by the Officers Warrant Officers and NCOs under his command who, during the grim struggle for existence against disease and starvation gave loyal support and assistance to maintain the Australian Forces as a well organized and well disciplined body of troops of an exceedingly high morale. In practicably no circumstance did this body of men fail to support the Commander, but rendered unselfish aid and encouragement to the men whose outlook at times looked hopeless. In the ranks of the men, too, were many hundreds who displayed the highest attributes and heroism, tenacity and comradeship in keeping with the best traditions of the AIF.

Time and time again there were examples of self-sacrifice and outstanding devotion to duty and to comrades which are too numerous for individual mention. There were, however, several exceptionally outstanding cases which it is considered are worthy of recognition by higher authority, and these form the subject of recommendations contained in Appendix VI to this report.

Conclusion

This report would not be complete without reference being made to the magnificent work performed by Lt-Col A Dillon MC 18 Div Headquarters. From the moment of his arrival at Banpong he grasped the seriousness of the situation and for eight months he hammered relentlessly at the representatives of the I.J.A. for improvements in conditions particularly so far as the sick were concerned. At no time did he consider the possible or probable consequences to himself resulting from the methods he adopted, but no matter how difficult the task might appear he devoted himself tirelessly to bringing about its fulfilment. Lt-Col Harris, The Commander of the Force, himself attributes to Lt-Col Dillon the praise and credit for any achievements gained for the Force as a result of the representations made to the I.J.A. by Force Headquarters from time to time.

Little remains to be said of this ill-fated Force. Almost from the beginning of this century a code of conduct, towards Prisoners of War, the aim of which has been to ensure their humanitarian treatment, has been adopted and faithfully carried out by practically all civilised nations. This code is embodied in the Geneva Convention of 1929. Although Japan was not a signatory to that convention she was a party to the Hague Convention of 1907, under which she, in common with other signatories, granted humanitarian treatment for Prisoners of War and promised, inter alia, to make adequate arrangements for the care of the sick, to treat Prisoners of War as regards rations, quarters and clothing on the same footing as her own troops, and not to employ them to excess. An examination of the previous pages of this report should leave no doubt in anyone's mind that not only had Japan broken her pledged word but by her barbarous conduct must forfeit any claims she may have held to be recognised as a civilized nation.

Every effort has been made throughout the compilation of this report to present the facts fairly and accurately. Whatever may be advanced in the future against any statements contained in the report the irrefutable fact remains and bespeaks its own story, that out of 6,999 men who comprised "F" Force 3,085 died, representing 44% of the original Force.

Signed at Changi, Singapore.
5th May, 1944
C.H. Kappe
C.H. Kappe Lt-Col
Commander, A.I.F. Component, "F" Force

Appendix I

To: Officer in Charge,
Shimo Songkurai Camp.

The medical situation in this camp is extremely grave and is becoming worse every hour. At the present moment cholera is raging – there have been 37 deaths and there are over 90 patients in hospital – new cases are occurring at the rate of 25 or more daily.

Dysentery is still a very serious problem and many men are so debilitated from prolonged dysentery or diarrhoea that it will be many weeks before they are fit for any form of work – meantime their resistance to cholera or any other disease is seriously impaired.

Malaria is rapidly increasing and we anticipate that within a week or two there will be hundreds of sufferers.

Taking this situation as a whole it is our anticipation that within one month there will not be 250 in this camp fit to do a day's work.

The reasons for this situation are that the men in this camp have been subjected to treatment which is wrong for any civilised nation to inflict on its Prisoners of War.

In detail:

i. The men before leaving Changi were weakened by dysentery and deficiency diseases (Beri Beri and Pellagra) and were in no condition to withstand infectious diseases.
ii. An assurance was given by the I.J.A. at Changi to the Commander A.I.F. that food would be better here than in Changi and that troops would not have to march from the railway to their destination. Neither of these promises have been kept. Relying on the second promise, many men totally unfit to march were included in the Force – very many of these men are now in hospital – some have died.

iii. The hygiene of the camps on the road was appalling and hundreds of men were successively infected by dysentery, by malaria and finally by cholera – the present tragedy is the result.

iv. The conditions of marching were extremely arduous and in some cases were unwarrantably cruel. Still men were driven out on to the road night after night, in some cases with high fever or active dysentery. As a result, when men arrived here, they were completely exhausted.

v. After arrival men were put in an unhygienic, badly situated camp, roofless and with very bad latrine accommodation; all conditions ideal for the spread of disease were present and disease has, in consequence, rapidly spread – your own report that 53 positive results for cholera were found shows how rapidly and wildly the spread took place.

vi. No adequate rest was given nor was any assistance given to requests for help. On the contrary men were sent to work and kept out of camp 12 and 13 hours a day in pouring rain – conditions typical not to the honourable treatment of Prisoners of War but slave labour.

At the present moment there are approximately:

37 men dead of cholera.

95 men in hospital with cholera.

250 men in hospital with other diseases.

140 men excused all duty on account of sickness – many of them would be in hospital if there were enough rooms or drugs or nurses.

150 men are so weakened by illness that they are only fit for light duties.

120 men being used (or have been used) in the case of the sick – of these 30 have already become so sick as to have been admitted to hospital. Thus about 800 men out of 2,000 have become invalids or have been required to nurse the sick within 14 days of the arrival of the troops in this camp – and the number is likely to increase rapidly.

In view of the above facts, we demand:

1. That this document be forwarded to the representative of the International Red Cross in Bangkok or Rangoon;
2. That all work shall cease not for 3 days, but indefinitely until the cholera epidemic has been got fully under control. In this circumstance we draw your attention to the promise given on 27th May 1943 that all work would cease for 3 days. This promise was broken the day after it was given. The reasons for asking for all work to cease are:
   i.   To enable hundreds of debilitated men to rest and recover their health.
   ii. To enable all necessary constructive work around the camp on latrines, roofing and drainage to be done.
   iii. To permit of enough men being allotted to nursing work to give adequate treatment to the hundreds of sick and the rest of the present over-worked and exhausted nursing staff.
3. The supply of adequate drugs, disinfectants, soap, lights and other medical supplies.
4. The supply of blankets for the sick.
5. The supply of invalid foods, soups, and tea and sugar for the sick.
6. The improvement of the camp diet by extra vitamin-containing food for example: - Rice polishings, towgay, meat, oil and fats.
7. The supply of suppressive atabrin for the whole camp – the present small quinine dosage is quite inadequate and without effect.
8. The supply of water containers, especially 44-gallon drums to enable water to be used on a large scale; also smaller containers for water boiling to make sterilization possible.
9. The supply of a large number of waterproof tents for the cholera area which is expanding daily. At least 30 large tents are required apart from what is now in the camp.
10. The supply of oil for dealing with mosquito breeding places in the camp – a visit from Capt. Wilson, Malaria expert at Headquarters Camp is urgently necessary to locate these.

11. The supply of protective clothing – white coats for nurses handling cholera.
12. As soon as the health of the camp has been improved, which may not be for several months, the evacuation of the area by troops and their subsequent treatment in a manner more befitting the honourable Japanese nation whose reputation must suffer gravely if the present conditions continue.

We demand that this document be laid before Lt-Col Banno and the senior Japanese medical officer for the area, and also before Lt-Col Harris at the earliest possible moment, preferably tonight.

Signed
N. McG. Johnston, Major, Commander AIF Troops Shino Songkurai Camp.
Bruce Hunt, Major, Senior Medical Officer.
C. Tracey, Major, Commander, No. 1 Bn.
R.H. Anderson, Major, Commander, No. 2 Bn.
Shimo Songkurai Camp,
30 May 43.

Appendix II

To: Lt-Col Banno,
Headquarters Camp,
Nieke
(through "F" Force Headquarters).

I wish to endorse the action of A.I.F. officers under my command who have deemed it necessary to submit a protest against the conditions to which the members of Changi "F" Force are being subjected. I forward herewith two further reports, one from Lt-Col Pond, Commander No. 4 Camp (in which I am quartered) and the other from Lieut Lillie, 2/29 Bn, who is in charge of personnel at the staging camp at Koncoita. These reports speak for themselves.

As commander of AIF personnel and as the senior Regular Australian Officer in Malaya I consider myself the representative of the Australian Government in this area and therefore respectfully submit that the following memorandum be passed to Lt-Col Banno for transmission to the International Red Cross.

In my considered opinion, which is supported by medical opinion, the present physical condition of the Force is such that in a few weeks there will be scarcely a man fit to carry out work of any nature and in addition the death rate is certain to increase. The men are so debilitated by the conditions of the long and arduous march of 280 kilometres through a series of insanitary staging camps that the majority have little physical resistance to diseases such as cholera, dysentery, severe diarrhoea, diphtheria, etc.

The food situation is serious. In 18 days, the men have had only rice and thin onion stew and occasionally beans and towgay. The quantity of the items is insufficient to maintain a reasonable standard of health. Two days ago, the rice ration was reduced from 4 to 3 bags for 700 men.

For three weeks there has been insufficient cover to protect the men from the rain which has fallen every day – on one occasion 230 men were completely soaked and another 200 men were unable to keep dry. Many men are obliged to sleep on the damp ground under the huts. Many have no boots at all, while some have boots which have little or no service left and badly need repairing. The supply and repair of footwear has been a problem since capitulation. Clothing is also urgently required, many men being in rags and several have little bedding. Considerable clothing had to be jettisoned by the men at Banpong to enable them to undertake the march to this area.

There is now a grave shortage of essential drugs. Requisitions have been submitted repeatedly but little relief has been given for the reason that the I.J.A. state they have no supplies. A requisition was submitted for extra food for the sick but I was informed that nothing could be done for even one sick man. Lately a small supply of tea and sugar has been made available for the dangerously sick cholera cases.

From the outset I have endeavoured to put my case to Lieut. Murayama. I made a request for an interview to discuss the question of accommodation for the sick, the food situation, the evacuation of the sick, canteen supplies etc. I have since submitted a further request for consideration of the food situation. To both of these I have received no acknowledgement – one was asked to be despatched to Lt-Col Banno if the local camp authorities could not act.

It was also pointed out that the digging of latrines to replace those already existing, which were conducive to the spread of disease, was delayed because all so-called fit men were required for road work. Whereas we were informed by the I.J.A. that they were moving "F" Force to an area where food was more plentiful, the reverse was the case.

On the grounds that the soldiers under my command, who fought honourably and well and who have been commended for their work and discipline, are not being treated in accordance with international agreements, I forward this request for investigation and necessary action by the International Red Cross.

I appreciate the problem of supply in an area with no railway and a bad road is immense, but the danger is great and the lives of many hundreds of men are at stake, particularly as the worst months of the monsoon are still to come. I am convinced that Lt-Col Banno is doing what he can to improve conditions but to my mind relief can only be obtained by reference to the highest authority.

(Signed) C.H. Kappe, Lt-Col,
Commander, AIF Troops "F" Force.

Appendix III

To Lt-Col Harris,
Headquarters Camp,
Nieke.

Protest regarding working conditions at No. 1 Camp.

It is again unfortunately necessary to lodge the most emphatic protest against the inhuman and barbaric conditions under which troops of this camp are being forced to labour in a manner much akin to slavery. It is felt that these conditions are intolerable, and were the full facts known in Tokyo they could not and would not be countenanced by such a nation as Japan, ranking as does that country among the Great Powers of the world.

Particular attention is drawn to the events of Tuesday 29th June although in making specific reference to that date it must be stressed that treatment accorded then merely represents a culminating point to which earlier working conditions have contributed. The various aspects are presented hereunder in summarised form.

1. Working Hours.
Working parties were handed over to the Engineers at 0900 hours and departed to work sites. Three parties comprising 120 men in all were engaged in putting down a corduroy road section. The outward trip was of about one hour's duration, over a distance of 4 kilometres. The work involved the cutting and carrying of heavy logs for which insufficient men were allowed. One rest period of 10 minutes was given during the morning between the hours of 1000 hours and 1215, when work ceased for lunch. No more than 30 minutes were allowed for the meal after which work resumed immediately.

Approximately half the men were given two or three rest periods during the afternoon, whilst the remainder were forced to labour without rest until 2100 hours. Owing to extreme darkness and the bad conditions of the road the return journey occupied ninety minutes and troops were not in camp until 2230 hours.

Thus, the men were absent from camp for periods up to 13½ hours and returned utterly exhausted nine hours after their lunch-time meal.

2. Severity of work.
As already mentioned, the work involved cutting and carrying heavy logs. The latter were anything up to 8 feet in length and 12 inches in diameter. Only five men were allowed to each log, and where these were smaller this number decreased to 3 or 4. A distance of approximately 400 yards was involved over a bad road in heavy mud and in practically incessant rain during the afternoon. Many of the men were without boots for which no replacements can be obtained and their feet were soon reduced to a bleeding and bruised condition. One man suffered injury when his foot was crushed by a log. Despite the fact that the sole of his boot was torn off and his foot badly bruised he was forced to continue working.

There were numerous cases of men exhausted by recent sickness being made to work without relief and all troops were continually harassed by back slapping and demands for more speed. A Sergeant was smacked about the face and neck for his inability to understand an order given in Japanese and even now is unaware of the nature of any offence. This incident was reported to the Engineer Corporal in charge but no action was taken.

Some parties, although told during the afternoon that they would be allowed to finish cutting 120 logs, were made to carry logs when cutting was completed despite the earlier promise.

3. Condition of Troops.
Attention is directed to the poor physical condition of men involved in road work. A large majority have been patients in hospital as sufferers from dysentery, malaria and other ailments since coming to this camp. Many were just released after long periods in hospital on a diet of 200 grammes of rice and have had neither time nor food to regain their strength. Others have worked incessantly on poor food and have had no rest days since their arrival unless actually in hospital as patients. All men leave camp soon after daylight and it is impossible for them

to attend to personal hygiene or even dry their soaking clothes under present conditions.

Considering the heavy work involved, these conditions are of appalling severity and could not even be expected of native coolie labour. It is intolerable that they should be imposed upon white troops – prisoners of war in the hands of a civilised and honourable power.

4. General Factors.

Attention is specially drawn to the following factors:

(a)   This camp is already supplying far greater numbers for work than any other camp of similar size or smaller in proportion.

(b)   The road section for which this camp is responsible is by comparison in a far better state than any other sections.

(c)   As a co-operative measure a test scheme involving the supervision and direction of qualified officers with troops under their own control was satisfactorily completed. Although this scheme was tried and found excellent from both points of view it has not been possible to arrange a conference to discuss its continuance or extension.

(d)   The demand for 300 workmen yesterday took practically every fit man in camp, despite the need to send a ration party of 50 men to No. 2 Camp. The latter party was finally made up of No Duty men, officers and permanent duties, involving much inconvenience in carrying on. Men on the ration party were required to carry an average load of 66 lbs at least and arrived back quite exhausted.

In general, it is felt that unless immediate steps are taken to alleviate these intolerable conditions any policy of moving sick men forward will only partially relieve local problems. Men cannot continue working thus without ruining their health and endangering their lives. Already Beri Beri, malaria and dysenteric relapses and sheer exhaustion are giving rise to a daily wastage well in excess of hospital discharges. Such a policy must inevitably mean reduced working parties and deterioration of the road upon which supplies and food depend.

In any event, intervention on the grounds of humanity alone is in every way justified and the strongest submission is made accordingly. This strong protest is being submitted direct to Force Headquarters as, despite urgent representations over recent weeks, it has apparently not been possible for the Camp Commander (Lieut Fukuda) to obtain any alleviation of conditions by negotiation with the local Engineers.

(Signed) N. McG. Johnston, Major, Camp Commander.
Shimo Songkurai Camp No. 1,
30 June 43.

Appendix IV

To: Lt-Col Banno,
I.J.A. Headquarters, Nieke.

I respectfully desire to bring to your notice the conditions of Australian soldiers in this camp and to request that sympathetic consideration be given to improving conditions.

1. The party under my command, originally 700, now consists of 523 of whom 37 are at Tamarumpat, and the balance are here. The party at Tamarumpat consists of men too sick to move and their number is decreasing by death every few days. They are without a medical officer and cannot obtain permission for nearby English and Australian doctors to visit them.
2. At Takakun there are 112 fit men, 19 light sick and 356 heavy sick men. Of the latter 58 are isolated with cholera. There have been 20 deaths from cholera in this camp but the epidemic now appears to be under control. I should like to express appreciation of the efforts made by the Japanese medical authorities to assist in checking this epidemic – they have been most helpful.
3. We were recently permitted to send 70 men to a hospital down river but there are at least another 185 men who should be evacuated to hospital as they will be unable to work for at least two months.
4. At the present I am required to send 200 men to work every day and also have to provide 20 cooks and 24 nursing orderlies. As a result about 120 heavy sick men have to go to work on the railway even though suffering from Beri Beri, Malaria and Dysentery. The work party leaves camp at about 0815 hours and returns usually about 2130 hours or later. The work is heavy, particularly in the almost constant rain and as a result sickness is increasing. I anticipate that if men with

heavy malaria and dysentery are to continue going to work many of them will die.

5. Of the men in this camp about 150 have no boots at all and over 150 have boots which are worn out beyond repair. The number of bootless men increases by about 30 per week. To provide boots for working men I took the boots of the men evacuated down the river to hospital. I have made several applications for an issue of boots but without success. Most of the men without boots now have large septic sores on their feet through having to work in continual wet and often on rocky ground and they endure great hardships. We also have 117 men without a shirt and 54 men without a pair of shorts, while 256 men have only one shirt and 317 have only one pair of shorts, 134 men have no towel and 181 have no ground sheets. Thanks to the issue by the I.J.A. all men now have a blanket.

6. Food has improved somewhat during the past three weeks but there is a serious lack of meat and fish. We have had meat on only five occasions in the last five weeks and that at the rate of 40, 55, 70, 80 and 40 grammes per man only. There has been no fish or meat even for working men in the past week – vegetables only. In English camps in this vicinity meat is issued daily at the rate of 200 grammes per man as well as vegetables and fish. We also need tea and sugar.

7. I have received orders that sick men in this camp are only to receive two meals a day and this order has been obeyed. I feel sure that as a result many of the sick men will not regain their health and strength and will not be able to work again. Some will no doubt die as a result.

8. Accommodation has improved a little with the building of three double-decker stages and with the evacuation of the 60 men to hospital but nevertheless most men become wet at night in bed when it rains as it does every night. In consequence the deaths of a number of men have really been caused by exposure.

9. I request that if this Force is required to move again some transport be provided for its baggage, tents, cooking utensils and rice, all of which have been required to be manhandled in the past. In my opinion, if this is not done, there will not be 100 men in the Force capable of doing any work after another move. Furthermore most of the sick men need transport though some would be able to march if they carried no baggage.

In conclusion, Sir, I trust that something may soon be done to improve the conditions of my men as I am very concerned at the number of deaths and the amount of sickness that have occurred.

I have the honour, etc.

(Signed) S.A.F. Pond, Lt-Col,
Commander A.I.F. Troops.
6th August, 1943

PS. Since writing this letter a further supply of meat at a generous scale has been received (120 grs) and we have been given to understand that this will continue regularly.

PPS. In reference to para 4 I should state that during the last two days the number of working men has not reached 200, but has been only from 140 to 175.

Appendix V

To: Lt-Col Banno,
I.J.A. Headquarters,
Nieke.

Sir,

I wrote a letter to you on 6th August and forwarded it to Lt-Col Kappe at Nieke for submission to you. The Sergeant of your guard at this camp has requested that I forward a report to you through him. I will therefore refer to my previous report and mention any changes in the position.

1. The party under my command is now 429, of whom 34 are at Tamarumpat. The party at Tamarumpat is still unable to get permission for a medical officer to visit them even though practically the whole party is sick.
2. The party here is divided in two, one party of 99 being about 2 kilometres away and the balance of 296 being here at Takanun.
3. Of the 393 men at Takanun, 153 are fit for work and 238 are sick and 44 are isolated with cholera.
4. We recently evacuated a further 80 men to a hospital at Tahso but at least another 100 and probably more should be evacuated as they will be unable to work for at least two months.
5. I am sending approximately 180-200 men to work every day and allowing for cooks and nursing orderlies this means that about 90 men who are sick are working each day. Owing to great urgency in completing the railway working hours have been longer, usually from 0815 to 2200 hours and sometimes to 0100 and 0300 hours.
6. The boot position has deteriorated as no boots have been received and additional boots have worn out. There are now over 150 men without boots. At least 300 pairs of boots are required. There

are approximately 40 men who have septic sores on the feet in consequence of having to work without boots. The clothing position is about the same, though some additional garments have worn out.

7. The food situation has improved somewhat as since 7th August meat has been received regularly though for the past ten days the quantity of meat received has been small and about 50 grs per man per day. The food received by the detached party of 99 men has been very good, both in meat and vegetables except dried potatoes for about two weeks. Men working late have on several occasions lately received milk from Japanese authorities items such as margarine and coffee These have been much appreciated.

8. Accommodation is still very unsatisfactory for though there is more room with the departure of some personnel tents are becoming rotten and incapable of repair and all leak badly. The detached party of 99 is well housed in attap huts.

9. I would like once more to stress the necessity for providing transport for all baggage if this party is required to move camp again. In my opinion there are only about 225 men in Takanun area who are in any way effective workers and I would respectfully request that only that number be required to do further work and that the balance of 170 here or evacuated to hospital down the river. The resistance of the men to disease is much impaired and I feel that further privations will greatly increase the rate of sickness. At the present time sickness has declined somewhat owing to improved food and the fact that canteen supplies can now be bought by the men – for which I am very grateful.

10. Owing to the cholera epidemic our men were until a day or two ago not permitted to wash in the river but had to carry filtered water some distance. As a result some men, particularly the very sick, have not been able to keep clean and some are infected with lice which are dangerous as giving rise to typhus.

11. I should like again to express appreciation of beef and supplies received from the Japanese medical authorities.

I have the honour, etc.

(Signed) S.A.F. Pond, Lt-Col,
Commander A.I.F. Troops Takanun.
24th August 1943.

Part II

Extracts of Unit Diary Maintained by Captain Ben Barnett

The following are extracts from the Unit Diary maintained by Captain Ben Barnett, Adjutant, 8 Division Signals, between April and October 1943. They are reproduced here courtesy of Wes Injerd, from the website www.mansell.com, who transposed it from the original file (reference number AWM 54 1010/4/10)

8 April

1700 hrs	Information received that a party of 7,000, including 3,300 A.I.F., would be moving north in about a week's time. Lt.Col. G.H. Kappe would comd the A.I.F. party. He wanted Capt. Stahl as his Staff Capt (A).
1945 hrs	Capt. Stahl attended conference at H.Q. 27 Bde. Indications are there will be approx. 5 offrs & 180 men from Signals in the party. All men to be fit, or nearly fit.

9 April

1715 hrs	Lt. Gawley attended conference at H.Q. Tech Regt. Return of no. of men available for Force "F" requested. No information about the number of men required from Signals yet available.
1000 hrs	Information received that 5 Signals offrs., Capt. Barnett, Lieuts. May, Stewart, Anderson and Henderson, will be proceeding north with Force F.
1030 hrs	All Group 2 (Light Duty) personnel re-classified as only fit, or nearly fit, will be moving with Force F.
1500 hrs	Capt. Barnett attended conference in connection with Force F. No definite figures yet available. Signals will form one Coy. in a Bn. commanded by Major Parry (A.A.S.C.). It is anticipated Force will commence to move on 17 or 18 APR.

There will be 12 trains, one per day, each carrying 580 or 590 troops. All personnel will be tested for dysentery & malaria. They will also be vaccinated and inoculated against cholera & plague prior to departure.

Indications are that we shall be moving to an unfurnished hutted camp about 5 days train journey from Singapore. All cooking gear will be taken.

11 April

1600 hrs	Capt. Barnett & Lieut. May attended conference at Regt. H.Q. Signals allotment of men for Force "F" is 219, comprising all fit (less 10), all Class 2, and 7 of Class 3 personnel. Signals will move in Train 4 – possibly on 21st or 22nd APR. I.J.A. want return of no. of men without mosquito nets (1), blankets (1) and singlets (1).
1900 hrs	After I.J.A. Check Parade, personnel concerned warned for move. Class 3 personnel had to be re-classified to enable 7 to be selected.
1930 hrs	Advice received that troops moving north would be vaccinated, inoculated and tested for malaria at 1400 hrs., 14 APR, on Barrack Square.

11 April

1000 hrs	Capt. Barnett & Lieut. May attended conference of [illegible] Bn. offrs. at House 42. Major Parry advised that latest information stated Force F was to be divided into 7 camps of 1,000 men.

14 April

	Indications are that feeding en route is good; but that drinking water has to be carefully watched.
	Only sufficient containers to feed men will be carried loose. The remaining cooking gear should be crated – if possible.
1400 hrs	Parade of Unit personnel moving north on Barrack Square for inoculations (cholera), vaccinations and malaria test.

15 April

1430 hrs	Parade of Unit personnel moving north on Barrack Square for glass rod (dysentery test) and inoculations (plague).

17 April

1000 hr	Warning Order that, if last night's I.J.A. order that all A.I.F. personnel have to move first is put into effect, Signals may have to leave Barrack Square at 0400 hrs tomorrow.

1400 hrs	Information received that Signals would be moving on Train 1 – i.e. 18 APR.
1430 hrs	Conference of offrs at H.Q. 27 Bde. Addressed by Lt. Col. Kappe. Party leaves Barrack Square at 0400 hrs. Assemble on Barrack Square 0230 hrs. 26 all ranks on trucks. 22 all ranks per train truck.

Cooks working all day and up to 2230 hrs preparing food for men to carry. Cooking gear then dismantled.

18 April

0100 hrs	Reveille. 0130 Breakfast. 0200 Fall in. Party, 5 offrs and 215 o/rs. moved to Barrack Square and were sorted into truck loads (alphabetically) by Div. H.Q. staff in teeming rain. I.J.A. trucks arrived fairly well on time – there were 14 of them for 600 men, their gear and all cooking gear for the force – and party proceeded in convoy to Singapore.

Each train load had its own medical supplies. There were 26 men to a railway truck. Trucks were small, metal and completely closed in except for two sliding doors in the centre, one on each side. It was impossible for all men to lie down at one time and tall men could not stand up straight. There were no conveniences of any description.

0650 hrs	Train left Singapore. An I.J.A. sergeant and about 15 guards were in charge of the party. Lunch, rice and vegetable stew was served at Gemas about 1500 hrs. Men had opportunities to purchase bananas & pineapples en route but were prevented from doing so in many instances by I.J.A. guards.

The absence of conveniences meant that at every stop men were relieving themselves at the side of the train, irrespective of where it was.

19 April

0300 hrs	Meal at Kuala Lumpur. Trip continued as for previous day with men taking every opportunity of washing themselves at engine supply points. A few men were hit by guards for getting out of the train before permission was given.

20-21 April   Still proceeding North in train.

22 April

1100 hrs   Arrived at BANPONG in Thailand and de-trained. Party moved to filthy camp about ¾ mile from station and there all men received stencilled I.J.A. number which was to be their identification for the next ten days. All gear had to be carried to the camp. This meant two trips back to the station for cooking gear.

It was learnt too, that the men now had a long march in front of them and the only gear that could be taken was that which could be carried. This was quite contrary to information given at Changi. Men immediately began to re-pack and sell anything that was not absolutely essential. Officers' trunks and cooking gear could not be taken.

These were left stacked, and W/O Allen (Engineers) was left behind to look after the gear and endeavour to get it transported to our final destination. The time of departure was originally given as midnight, but this was subsequently changed to 24 hours later. After the evening meal, then men had an impromptu concert and then a good night's sleep.

23 April   Men continued to reduce amount of kit.

1200 hrs   Train load No. 2, including Lt. Col. Kappe, Capt. Stahl & Capt. Hargrave, arrived. Their experience had been similar to ours.

2230 hrs   Fall in for Train No.1. 2330 hrs. I.J.A. check.

24 April

0030 hrs   Party moved off on start of 24-kilometre march. March table was 40 mins march, 20 mins rest. Hot water was provided after about 10 kilos. Destination was reached at about 0930 hrs.

We had to provide our own cookers to prepare meals (breakfast, rice & a small piece of dried fish had been carried on the man). Men welcomed a swim in nearby river. They were also permitted to trade with natives and consumed large quantities of eggs, coffee etc. to supplement rice & stew.

In view of the strenuous nature of the march and the possibility that it was to continue for several days, men were allowed to consume the reserve rations they had brought from Changi.

2130 hrs   Fall in 2230 hrs. Move off on next stage of march. Distance approx. 25 kilos. Hot water was provided after about 14 kilos and men had an hours rest. At [illegible], our doctors' dais there were 42 men who were too sick to proceed. This number the I.J.A. reduced to 10. The others had to march.

Here, too, we were fortunate enough to hire a hand cart to transport the medical paniers which had been carried by the men on the previous night. At the halfway halt, the sick were again inspected and the I.J.A. allowed another 6 or so to be transported.

25 April

0930 hrs   Arrived at halt No.3. Only covering was one shelter for cooks, R.A.P. and offrs. All o/rs. slept in open or under trees.

Men were permitted to swim in river about 1 mile away, proceeding there in organised parties under I.J.A. guard.

Night spent at this camp – KANCHAN BURI.

26 April

0930 hrs   Train load No.2 personnel arrived.

1400 hrs   Our party proceeded to I.J.A. hospital about 3 kilometres away where we received blood test, dysentery test (glass rod) and two inoculations (cholera & fever).

2130 hrs   Fall in for next stage of journey – approx. 20 kilos. During this stage we left the good roads and proceeded along bush tracks. At halt No.3, medical stores had been broken up and given to individuals with the exception of 2 paniers. This made carriage much easier.

26 April

0900 hrs   Arrived at halt No.4. Best camping spot to date, right on river with facilities to purchase from natives.

27 April

2100 hrs   Fall in. Check and then start on next stage – approx. 22 kilo.

Hot water at halfway house, and hours rest.

28 April

0830 hrs   Arrived at halt No.5, about ¼ mile from river.

Policy was adopted of putting men with sore feet etc. into the cookhouse to enable them to obtain a few days' rest. No experience is needed for cooking plain rice and a stew consisting of onions and a little whitebait.

Independent swimming was permitted, and men were allowed to trade with natives. Prices were getting higher, however, and variety of goods very limited. Night 28-29 Apr. spent at this halt.

29 April

0730 hrs   Train load No.2 arrived.

1930 hrs   Fall in and start on next stage – approx. 24 kilos.Water at halfway house and an hour's rest. Fortunately, up to this stage we have had no rain during our marches and marching at night is much preferable to marching in the heat of the day. We had a few hours rest and a sleep just before dawn.

30 April

0830 hrs   Arrived at halt No.6, TARSO. This is a big base camp and here we met Capt. Newton and a number of "D" Force. As usual, cooks & sick personnel were left by us.

1930 hrs   Fall in and start on next stage – another 20 kilos. Hot water & rest at halfway house.

1 May

0630 hrs	Arrived at halt No.7. Spent the day resting. No natives with whom to trade. It was in flat swamp by small creek.
1900 hrs	Fell in, check and again onwards. Nobody left at this camp. Just after we started, it rained heavily. Track was very muddy and slippery and going was bad.

2 May

0530 hrs	Arrived at halt No.8 & spent 2 hours sitting on road waiting to be checked. This site is near another large camp. We swam in the river about 1 kilo away; but opportunity for local purchases were few. Camp was named KENSIOKE. Spent night 2/3 May here.

3 May

0530 hrs	Train load No.2 arrived.
1900 hrs	Fall in, check, move off. After about 10 kilos halted for 1 hour. It rained and we proceeded in heavy rain. Track very slippery, steep and dark. Progress for next hour extremely hard and slow.

4 May

0830 hrs	Arrived at halt No.9. Camp near creek & plenty of trees for shelter. Day spent resting. 1930 hrs. Fall in and moved off on next stage.

5 May

0830 hrs	Arrived at halt No.10. I.J.A. guards strict. 20 offrs allotted to 1 tent. Men in open. Good swimming in river 100 yards off. Day spent resting. Tenko at 2030 hrs. Night 5/6 May spent at this camp. No opportunity for private purchase.

6 May

1900 hrs	Fall in and proceed on next stage. Rain and heavy going for portion of journey.

7 May

0830 hrs   Arrived at halt No.11 – about 2 kilometres beyond SANK(C) BURI which is 207 kilometres from BAN PONG. Were given 3 meals here instead of usual 2, and for evening meal one small tin of whale meat was issued to every 10 men. Only a mouthful, but very acceptable. The neighbouring creek was shallow but good for washing. Here supplies of chloride of lime petered out and orders were issued that in future all drinking water had to be boiled. Men rested during the day.

1900 hrs   Fall in. The next stage is 26 kilometres, so we were told. After marching about 5 kilos, halted outside camp where Norfolk Regt. were in residence. Their food during that time had been rice & onions & whitebait stew, with no opportunity for canteen purchases.

8 May

0530 hrs   Arrived at halt No.12 – TARRA ROMPAT. It could not have been more than 20 kilos from TARRACOON, our last halt. Men slept 'till 0800 hrs. Then tenko. This camp appears to be an I.J.A. stores centre. Good swimming in river 150 yards away. Men also collected large clams in stream and supplemented their diet … Spent night 8/9 MAY here.

9 May

0800 hrs   No.2 party arrived. No.1 party was warned to be prepared to move at any time during day. R.C. and C. of E. church parades were arranged for 1600 hrs, but these had to be cancelled owing to an I.J.A. tenko being called at that time.

1930 hrs   A party of 700, consisting of 253 of No.1 party (party 1 included 120 sigs) – which had been re-organised into Units in place of Companies of numbers been two consecutive hundreds – and 447 of No.2 party fell in and moved off on next stage. We were told this stage was to be only 10 kilometres. After marching for about 16 kilometres, we were given 3 hours rest, then march continued. Only a very limited supply of water was available.

10 May

0930 hrs   Arrived at halt No.15 - KONKOITA – approx. 24 kilos from TARRA ROMPAT. Men were left sitting in the sun by the river until after lunch (1230 hrs). No swimming was permitted. Then party moved to un-roofed huts. A limited number of tents were supplied to provide covering. Offrs. & men were very cramped. Good swimming in river 50 yards away but no opportunity for local purchase. It was anticipated this was to be the base camp. Tea or coffee have by this time become most precious. None is supplied by I.J.A. whose other rations are unchanged. Men spent night 10/11 here.

11 May

1000 hrs   Warning Order that Signals, less 16 cooks, Sigmn Lowe (interpreter) & Sigmn [illegible] (batman to Lt. Col. Kappe) would be prepared to move at 1230 hrs. Distance 7 kilometres. Task, bridge building.

1300 hrs   Signals (6 offrs. & 99 o/rs.), Capt Mills (M/O) and one med. orderly left camp. 12 of our sick personnel were transported by truck.

1600 hrs   Arrived destination. Settled in roofless hut. 3 tents erected to provide partial covering (TAIMONTA).

12 May

0930 hrs   Started work. 3 parties provided … 2 offrs & 29 o/rs, 2 offrs 29 o/rs, 2 offrs 25 o/rs. Other personnel Cooks 6, R.S.M., Hygiene Sgt, sick 8, R.M.O., Med Ord. Lunch 1330 – 1530 hrs. Men finished work 2045 hrs.

13 May   Information is that bridge approx. 70 feet, is to be finished in 5 days.

14 May   Parties unchanged. O/C, Capt. Barnett, saw Capt. MURIAMA regarding better food for men and also requested only 1 offr. be allocated to each party. People in sick bay at tenko is now 18.

15 May	Sick now 21. Work parties unchanged, with exception that only one officer per party now goes out.
16 May	Still on bridge. Sick 25. Rations – rice & thin onion stew. Balance of No.1 Party and No.2 Party moved up from KONKIOTA owing to cholera scare. Shifting Unit quarters cancelled night work we were supposed to do.
17 May 2130 hrs	Sick still mounting, now 31. Mostly diarrhoea & beri-beri. All Unit personnel again inoculated against cholera. News was received today that there was cholera in 2/30 Bn camping up river. 10 cases 1 death. Three doctors = Major Hunt, Major Stevens & Capt Hendric – sent forward.
18 May	Men on bridge working until 2045 hrs. A hard afternoon finding & cutting logs.
19 May	Morning task – cutting logs for decking of bridge. Afternoon half holiday. Lieut Anderson off colour for last few days … One officer resting. About 40 men sick.
20 May	Still on bridge. Same no. off colour. Mess still rice onion stew but men gathering greens & doing a little private cooking. Wet night. Most men got wet. Gear also.
21 May	Rain during afternoon.
22 May	Wet all day. Miserable working conditions.
23 May	Again wet. A lot of men had no dry clothes to wear but they were generally cheerful. In view of rain, work ceased at 1745 hrs. Still cutting timbers for a new bridge and clearing scrub around creek.
24 May 2100 hrs	No work in morning owing to wet state of ground. A/ RSM reported spirit of unrest among some of the men. Check parade & men addressed by Lt.Col. Kappe on futility of escape.

25 May

0900 hrs   SX7592 L/Cpl Miller C.G., VX32772 Sigmn Benoit M.A.W. and SX7220 Sigmn Seymour E. absent from Work Parade. Matter reported to I.J.A. Fine in morning, rain during afternoon. Me working until 2020 hrs.

26 May   All party placed in quarantine owing to a suspected cholera case.

0845 hrs   Approx. man died. No working parties.

27 May   Still in quarantine. As there is no work, mess reduced to gruel (rice boiled twice, which reduces quantity) and the same with stew.

1900 hrs   Second man from 2/29 Bn died.

28 May

0715 hrs   I.J.A. sentries saw man with uncooked rice in a bag. They did not catch him, but they said there would be no breakfast until he owned up.

0830 hrs   Muster parade for inspection by I.J.A. sentries. Unit hut inspection looking for food.

1500 hrs   Breakfast as man admitted guilt. 1800 hrs. "Lunch". 2200 hrs. Evening meal ... injections for cholera recommenced.

29 May   Still in quarantine & rations of gruel & onion water. Very little salt in food. A few decent fish have been caught recently & "greens" – boiled centre of banana palms have been popular. Ground still very muddy but sun for a short time during the day has enabled men to so some drying out. Information is that trucks are bogged all along the road.

Our sick figures today 2 offrs (Anderson & Henderson) 43 o/rs. no duty, 12 o/rs. light duty, 13 o/rs. in hospital. All of these are dysentery or diarrhoea, fever, beri-beri, or tropical ulcers. Three men ... & the two Arrowsmiths volunteered as orderlies in dysentery & cholera wards. Another death today from cholera (2/10 Engineers). I.J.A. have forbidden washing, swimming & fishing in the creek. All water must be carried to lines.

30 May

0930 hrs   Capt. Hardacre set out for No.3 camp, 16 kilos further on, on errand for Lt.Col. Kappe. 1030 hrs. … All dysentery cases concentrated in one hut. 1900 hrs. Information that for next four days, we will only receive one (1) bag of rice for all troops (about 700) & this will be served in two meals … 1½ bags of rice received, but only 2 meals – 1130 hrs & 1330 hrs. …

1 June   Lieut Anderson still in dysentery isolation. Lt Stewart fever. Sigmn Morrison improved …

2 June   Wet. One coy of 2/29 Bn had a YAK. Still on 2 meals a day – gruel and thin, very thin, stew supplemented by banana stalks.

3 June   Wet. Informed that all fit men had to go out to work today.

4 June   Evidently I.J.A. has decided that cholera precautions no further necessary. Total party 235 – 9 offrs & 226 O/Rs (4 Sigs offrs & 28 O/Rs). Working men to receive 3 meals & … rice, Task – removing mud from approaches to bridges up to 3 kilos from camp and replacing with creek soil.

It was an extremely difficult walk along terribly muddy road to the job. Then continuous rain practically made the task impossible. Furthest men out did not get back to camp until about 2100 hrs. Japs killed yak & gave us 6 lbs meat … From another one (un-official) Unit in lines … received 22 lbs.

5 June   Wet again, but still work parties required. Task making & levelling roads. Rain made it impossible to complete task in time.

Another cholera case (Engineers) … Warning Order that all fit men would be moving to another camp & carrying gear & tents – 10 kilometres from here. Out of 81 men in lines, only 44 say they could make the trip.

6 June   Wet.

1000 hrs   Work levelling road.

1215 hrs   All men recalled to camp for another dysentery test (glass rod) … Movement of fit men postponed a day … More yak.

7 June   Work only in morning until it rained. Afternoon "off" in view of movements. Unit did well (privately!) in yak killed by I.J.A. …

8 June

1045 hrs   Party moved out. Yak carts carried tents & cooking gear. Word received from party passing through that VX 32432 Sigmn Griffiths G.T.S. had died somewhere back along the road. Main party left him at BANPONG suffering from scrotum trouble. Sick personnel have been back on 3 meals a day – plain rice and very watery "stew" – since 6 JUN.

9 June   Fine morning … Wet afternoon. Midday meal, gruel only – no stew … Two yaks – neither official – cheered men. One 2/29 Bn man died of malaria.

10 June   A fine day. The first day without rain for some time … Men returned with 5 yaks. … All personnel from this camp to move on shortly.

11 June   Another fine day. Men here still on 3 meals a day with occasional yak stew. Warning Order that 2 offrs and 68 o/rs all "fit" will be moving on.

12 June

0945 hrs   Lieuts Anderson & Brindley (Engrs) with 68 o/rs marched out carrying gear, midday meal – 23 ozs. dry rice per man (rations until & incl. midday meal 13 JUN) … cooking containers, & 3 tents less sides & ends (the I.J.A. insisted these tents be carried despite the fact that the men are in a weakened state.) At the last moment, each man was given a chunkel (a kind of improvised pick-axe) to carry …

0100 hrs   VX 43916 Miller M.J. transferred to cholera isolation. He died later in the day at 1645 hrs here at TAIMONTA, THAILAND. He had been ill with dysentery for some time – in fact, he had not been really well since we left Changi.

1000 hrs   Capt Browning & 14 o/rs … left for KONKOIDA to collect sugar & coffee for us – so they were told by I.J.A. doctor here. 1815 hrs. Party returned with sugar & coffee (mostly for the nips) & I.J.A. clothing. Rain today, but not till afternoon …

13 June   Sigmn Miller cremated. Another cholera case (Engineers). Camp again placed in quarantine. Japs gave us 15 ½ lbs of sugar and 6 lbs of coffee …

14 June   Fine until about 1800 hrs. Wood & greens party. Mens' health improving.

15 June   Party of 20 o/rs (1 sigmn) to KONKOIDA. Collected 7 cases of 24 – 2 ½ lb. tins of tongue and 2 other cases, none received by us. Warning Order that further party of 2 offrs & 90 o/rs – fit men – moving on tomorrow.

16 June
0950 hrs   Party under Capt. Curlewis moved out carrying tents, Jap cases, & rations for 2 days. Signals personnel left at TAIMONTA now 1 offr (Capt. Barnett, fit) and 40 o/rs (2 fit, 8 no duty, 13 light duty, 13 hospitalised, 4 cooks). Fine morning, wet afternoon.

17 June
1900 hrs   Lieuts Vietch (A.A.M.C.) arrived back from NICKAYE with quinine. He reported Lt.Col. Kappe & party were camped 1 kilometre from NICKAYE and were under 3 hours' notice to move back to TAMARUMPET about

50 kilos back. Their task of bridge building & road making is NOT nearly half complete. Reason, shortage of rations.

18 June   Information that all our party, 700 strong originally, will be moving back. No definite date of our departure. Japs state, strongly, that we shall all shortly be returning to Malaya.

19 June   Fine most of day. 1230 hrs. Lt.Col. Kappe arrived. Remainder of his party 409 strong & well laden with tents & rations kept arriving until about 1900 hrs. They spent night 19/20 here. 19 Signals were left behind at hospital at NICKAYE. There are 5 offrs (Capt. Hardacre, Lieuts May, Stewart, Henderson & Anderson) & 51 o/rs in this party.

They had been better off than us for rations, rice averaging about 1 lb. per man per day and plenty of yak (meat). Additional rice could also be bought. We are now down to 11ozs. per man per day – i.e. 1 pint cup of gruel 3 times a day. [illegible] bought some rice from the party & Capt Barnett was [illegible] seaweed.

20 June
1015 hrs   Lt.Col. Kappe's party moved out for KONKOIDA, party of 130 returned in the afternoon to carry nips' stores ... Warning Order that all of our party would be moving back to KONKOIDA tomorrow. Very sick will have to be carried. As a result of our purchases from this other party, we had 3 adequate meals today ...

21 June   Reveille 0745 hrs. Breakfast 0815 hrs. Tents struck, gear packed and party carrying [lunch?] ready to move by 1100 hrs. Approx 150 men from Lt.Col. Kappe's party arrived from KONKOIDA to assist in transport of our gear & sick personnel. Only one of our men Sigmn GYNAN carried on stretcher ...

Party eventually left at 1300 hrs. & completed arrival at KONKOIDA by about 1700 hrs, distance 7 kilometres. Rain after we had proceeded about halfway made bad track very slippery.

22 June

0900 hrs   All fit men of both parties (182) returned to TAIMONTA to collect Jap stores. Most loads were too heavy for men not 100% fit. Wire, axes, picks, chunkels, tents had to be carried … Japs insisted on a second trip being made. Would NOT let unfit men drop out after first trip, with exception of 13. Reinforcements of 45 men obtained.

Second carry was heavier than first, and a heavy shower just before we left TAIMONTA made track very difficult … Last men arrived back at KONKOIDA after being reinforced by additional volunteers over final kilometre, at 2145 hrs. Two hard trips knocked up many men …

23 June

0900 hrs   Another party of fit men to TAIMONTA … to assist in towing back 2 Jap trucks & staff car. All day task. Information received that complete party would be moving back another 8 kilometres tomorrow. Lt. Col. Kappe & Sigmn Duesberry would be returning to NICKAYE and Lt. Col. Pond would be re-assuming command of our personnel.

24 June

0700 hrs   Reveille.

0800 hrs   Breakfast. Party ready to move by 0900 hrs. All our tents and cooking gear had to be carried. Last men moved out at 1100 hrs. Rain made road very slippery & muddy. Arrival at new camp about 1700 hrs.

Party had to move back immediately to assist stretcher cases – one man developed cholera en route – another party under Capt Hardacre went back to pull out yak carts carrying Jap personal gear. Japs arrived at midnight & said tea must be sent out to these men (2 offrs 25 o/rs). They eventually arrived back about 0800 hrs on 25 Jun having left carts still stuck about 4 kilometres from here.

25 June

0700 hrs   Orders to move fit men to TAMARUMPET & sick another 7 kilometres (approx. ½ way) suspended owing to non-arrival of yak carts. Men were all packed in anticipation of move but at 0945 hrs. move back was cancelled and all fit & light duty ordered back to assist in movement of these carts. 1730 hrs.

All men who could walk & carry gear ordered to move to next camp 7 ½ kilos away. Yak party sent back to carry tools & Jap gear to their camp. They set out about 1845 hrs & arrived back up to early hours 26 Jun. Party with gear left about 1930 hrs. Another 2/29 man died of cholera.

26 June   Another cholera death (2/29) early hrs morning. Party remaining at this camp (approx. 400) started to move off from KRIEN KRIE [?] at 0930 hrs. Men could not carry all tents & had to lift them by [illegible].

It was anticipated party would only be moving 7½ kilos but they were sent straight through to TARRARUMPET. Track was very bad & wet in afternoon. Several men could NOT make distance & slept by side of track. All stretcher parties (8) except 1 got through, but men had a terrible job & only made the grade because of assistance sent out from first party. Many tents dumped after 3 ½ kilos & a number more at half-way point. At TARRUMPET there was no camp [illegible] & most men slept in open ...

27 June   Several cases of cholera developed after the extremely difficult move ... Party of 230, fit & light duties, sent out without breakfast to 7½ kilos camp to collect tools.

1800 hrs   Party of 50 had to move to river 1 kilo away to carry rice. Four trips were necessary & it became increasingly difficult to obtain reliefs. Owing to difficulty of recovering [illegible] individuals some days ago, most men were on 2 meals only.

28 June   Rice issue of I.J.A. approx. 18 ozs per man per day. Men working carrying logs for small bridge & levelling road. Party of 30 o/rs went back to collect remaining tents … Light duties used for collecting bamboo for tent flooring & for carrying rations (vegetables) from river 1½ kilos away. Men permitted to trade with vendors in camp area & could purchase guala malacca [local sugar], [illegible], tobacco … Roads wet & slippery. Further two cholera suspects …

29 June   Fit total 104. 20 men under Lieut Henderson went back for final lift of tents. Capt Muriama gave permission for 1 offr to go across to kampong with I.J.A. soldier to make purchase of coffee, soap & guala malacca for R.A.P. … Task for fit men – road levelling.

　　　　　Men were dismissed early – about 1745 hrs. Light duties still collecting bamboo & food. Another cholera death … (Evening mess for Lt. Col. Pond & me – rice, jungle stew, beans, seaweed … with guala malacca & tea) …

30 June   No men on road. Further purchases O.K. from neighbouring kampong.
1300 hrs   Rumours of further move in 2 days' time …

1 July
0845 hrs   Definite order that all fit & light sick would be moving back tomorrow. Heavy sick will remain. Approx is that 360 move (at 0800 hrs) & remainder 270 odd stay.
12.15 hrs   Lt. Col. Pond saw Capt Muriama. All men must eventually move within few days. Five days rice will be allowed total party. 360 fit moving carry 3 days rice for journey = 25 kilometres to TAKANOON in 3 stages of approx. 8 kilos … Nips gave us 449 blankets today. Only 237 were required but they insisted we take the lot.

2 July

0915 hrs   Party of 356 ... moved off, very heavily laden, 272 all ranks left at Tameron Park (TARRUMPET) under Major Parry. Party moved approx. 7 kilos on dry track, then lunched & moved on. Passing cliffs where blasting was in progress, it would have been impossible to manhandle stretchers. It is to be hoped sick will be transported by barge as indicated by Japs.

2030 hrs   Pitched camp for night after walking 14 kilos. Tough going. ...

3 July

1000 hrs   Moved on. The fact that we had only 1½ kilos to go was a pleasant surprise. Pitched camp on hill at TAKANAN. No huts. No latrines but close to good creek. Capt MURIAMA informed Lt Col Pond we would be here for 2 months working on the railway. Rumours were strong at all camps en route that all Europeans would be out of Thailand by the end of this month and the railway completed by Asiatic labour.

On arrival at camp site, all personnel started settling in but at 1400 hrs Nip [ordered?] all fit men required as carrying party. ...

2000 hrs   Capt Barnett, Hardacre & Lt May dined with Maj Thyer (Malayan Cmd Sigs) at neighbouring camp. Best meal since leaving Changi, and plenty of it – rice & veg soup, meat rissole & greens, jam ...

4 July

0900 hrs   All fit men (100) to work. Lt Col Pond saw Capt Muriama who stated all light sick must also work. This party (65) moved off with Capt Hardacre about 1030 hrs after much flashing of a stick by a Jap. Task building latrines at a new Jap camp adjoining our area ... Today, 'no duty' men had to work around Unit lines clearing scrub, erecting bamboo [illegible] etc. for tents.

5 July	New timetable. Men have to work 12 hrs a day. Fall in 0800 hrs & return to camp about 2030 hrs. or when they complete a set task. One group of 4 men have to move [illegible] cub. metres of earth per day, 5 party of 2 carry 250 loads of earth. Work is in railway cutting. Light duty men working around new Jap camp. 15 of these in Jap cookhouse.
1400 hrs	Personnel from Tameron Park began to drift in. Party of 225 arrived during the afternoon. 48, sick 43 med personnel 5, only men left at Tameron Park. Signal personnel … party of 223 left on 4 Jul & had strenuous trip. Majority of them unfit. They carried tents, cooking gear, etc.
6 July	195 fit & light duty personnel out to work. 'No duty' men building fence around area. Latrines poor & fouled. 'No duty' personnel have to attend to all camp hygiene …
2000 hrs	Further glass rod test tomorrow. Working men will NOT go out until after test but must dig new latrines & clean up camp area beforehand.
7 July	
0830 hrs	Fit men started on latrines. Light duty men on cleaning up lines.
1000 hrs	Glass rod test for cholera. Total no. (580) O.K. at first count.
1200 hrs	Working men moved out, 16 short of early morning count. Capt MURIAMA came down to camp & told Lt Col Pond he had lied about figures & paraded all [illegible] cases. He was satisfied they could NOT work. First choleras case in this camp today.
8 July	Interference by several I.J.A. privates in dividing up working parties considerably delayed departure of workers. Light duties working in same parties as fit men. Lt Col Pond had long talk to Capt MURIAMA … He promised to help light duties personnel [illegible] in future, look into matter of improved rations & canteen … 190 all ranks

	to work today. 'No duties' cleaning up camp & digging latrines.
1900 hrs	Cpl … died of cardiac beri-beri. He was a post-cholera case.
2100 hrs	Capt MURIAMA gave Capt Barnett authority to operate canteen [illegible] English Camp through authorised Chinese vendor.

10 July	Two more deaths this morning … both malaria. Another cholera case (2/29) too. A further 2 deaths this afternoon … a bad day.
1730 hrs	Five bodies cremated on one pyor [pyre].
1830 hrs	Further glass rod test for all personnel …
2115 hrs	Lt Col Pond & Capt Barnett saw Capt MURIAMA. He was most affable & listened to our requests for meat, rice polishings, changing of Malayan currency. We were given a favourable hearing on all counts.

Rations are improving. Plenty of rice (about 24 ozs per day per man) and excellent issue of vegetables & dried fish. Also 21 tins of coconut oil & 8 cases of tinned herrings left at [illegible] store. We understand the latter is for us.

11 July	Wet morning after wet night. Only 118 o/rs (fit 83, light duties 35) available for work out of 546. Cholera cases still increasing & a further "Glass Rod" test for all ranks at 1800 hrs.

12 July	In quarantine. No movement out of camp area without I.J.A. authority. Men working on railway at camp boundary and without strict I.J.A. supervision.

Rations: approx. 24 ozs rice, 30 ozs vegetables, some dried fish per man per day. I.J.A. arranged Malaysian currency exchange dollar for dollar.

Cholera NOT abating. Late start at work owing to heavy rain early. Men working until 2200 hrs on railway. Another death …

13 July

1700 hrs   Personnel whose cholera test was positive re-tested. As tests from 3 men went into one test tube, this meant re-testing of 63 men all of whom have to be isolated …

14 July

1100 hrs   Work on railway stopped by Capt MURIAMA to enable men to complete bamboo flooring for tents – difficulty was collecting suitable bamboo – drainage camp area completely, latrines etc.

All of this work should have been done in first few days at this site, but no respite was allowed after our hard march & all fit and light duty personnel had to go out to work next day.

Three signals to cholera isolation today …

15 July   A fine morning. Men concentrating on tent flooring & cleaning of additional area for cholera isolation. There are now 32 patients isolated … 1500 hrs men – fit and light duties – started work on railway. Worked until 2000 hrs. …

16 July

0800 hrs   Work again. 20 men allowed for work at cholera isolation. Capt Muriama NOT receptive to repeated requests for meat. All tent floorings finished but many have to be improved …

1700 hrs   Yet another cholera test – glass rod – all ranks.
Some cooks 'bashed' by Capt MURIAMA for fishing in creek.

17 July   Capt Muriama would not let party of light duty finish huts in cholera area. All must work on railway. Officers i/c parties given labouring jobs … Only very few men (Signals – 18) fit for working parties today. Wet day but no rest from work. New KOREAN guards took over from Sgt

SHINAHARA's party who set out for NICKAYE. Extra rations of fish for workers.

18 July   Wet morning. Total working on railway 5 offrs 103 o/rs. … Capt MURIAMA would NOT allow party to assist cholera in [illegible] & erecting of tents. Capt Mills moved all A.A.M.C. personnel to cholera area & got volunteer 'no duty' personnel …) to look after hospital in this area. 45 men (9 groups of 5) to be re-tested for cholera …

19 July   Only 63 o/rs fit for work. Instruction received from Capt MURUYAMA that we had to supply 130 o/rs and 7 offrs. 'No duty' personnel were paraded by coys and Capt Mills indicated those most fit to make up number. Neighbouring creek has risen about 20 feet & cookhouse had to be moved. 5 [illegible] for rice cooking received – thank heaven.

1630 hrs   Further request from I.J.A. of no. of men who would NOT be able to work within a month. They are to be sent back to hospital at KANBURI.

20 July   A fine day. 131 o/rs at work 8 offrs. Three more men (all 2/29) died of cholera during early morning. Conditions at isolation area very bad & no fit or light duty personnel allowed to assist in improving. Workers had lunch & tea out & were informed they would have to work through night until set task finished. They were eventually knocked off at 2245 hrs. I.J.A. provided meat – the first for ages – for yak stew for midnight meal for workers. 1600 hrs. Further cholera test for 45 suspected carriers. Previous test ruined at laboratory.

21 July   Workers 8 offrs 100 o/rs. New task – clearing yak yard & cutting timber to improve rd.

1130 hrs   All men called back to camp. All tents vacated & sprayed by I.J.A. with disinfectant. Then Capt MARUYAMA supervised break up into fit, light duty & heavy sick areas …

1330 hrs	All fit & light duty personnel in camp again tested for cholera (glass rod). Information that party had to move up to TARRUMPET to bring back tents & any sick who can move tomorrow & return 23 JUL. Order cancelled later. Also rumour that fit men will move to new camp about 200 yards away – in a yak yard. 50 men sent in afternoon to clear area & carry saplings to corduroy road …
22 July	Only 50 workers required. Task – clearing yak yard.
1200 hrs	Further cholera test for fit and light duty personnel. All Signals in cholera isolation progressing satisfactorily.
23 July	Wet. Conditions bad. All fit & light duty personnel working on yak yard. Still in bad condition.
1200 hrs	Men classed as fit & light duty had further cholera test.
1700 hrs	All 'no duty' personnel & men in isolation & hospital tested for cholera …
24 July	Very wet. Stream still rising. Two cooks allowed to operate filter … All fit & light duties again working on railway line (2 offrs 68 o/rs).
1030 hrs	Capt Barnett saw Capt MARUYAMA regarding possible move of fit – no time set out yet, but after results of cholera tests – pay – nothing definite but only for workers. Cremations – O.K. without referring to him …
25 July	Padre Babb & Capt H Lord from English Camp about 2 kilos away still doing magnificent job supplying our lads with canteen goods, carrying them down themselves & delivering to our working party.
1700 hrs	Word received that party of 70 sick men would be moved down to river by barge to WYNYEA [railhead near TARSO] leaving at 0900 hrs 26 JUL … All party again tested for cholera. Time of departure later altered to 0800 hrs and then 0730 hrs. Fit men building staging at new area. Then moved after mess.

26 July

0630 hrs   Reveille.

0745 hrs   Party of 3 offrs & 67 o/rs moved off. Creek still over road bridge. All who could had to cross by railway bridge. Others, including 4 stretcher cases, taken across by boat ...

Officers built double decker staging in "fit" area & shifted after mess ... 2 further cholera deaths. "Unfit" area only on 2 meals today.

27 July   2 offrs 54 o/rs fit for work. Capt MARUYAMA ordered 10 offrs & 150 men out. All fit & light duties from "unfit" area (including suspected cholera cases in isolation) and 17 'no duty' from "fit" area ordered out. Just enough. "Unfit" area, including workers & hospital orderlies, still on 2 meals only. Capt MARUYAMA would NOT listen to protest.

28 July   Nos for work same as yesterday, but owing to these suspected cholera carriers in "unfit" area being definitely excluded, we could only supply 10 offrs & 106 men.

0930 hrs   Further cholera test for all fit men in "unfit" area. Cookhouse complete shifted to fit area. Capt Barnett received excellent "bashing" from 2 Korean guards for referring to them to Sgt ITO as "KOREANS". Padre Dodds & Capt Lord still supplying us with canteen supplies from English camp. Task for all parties – fit, light duties & offrs – 450 baskets.

29 July   Nos for work 10 offrs 106 o/rs.

30 July

1030 hrs   Capt Barnett visited English camp with authority from Capt MARUYAMA asking for medical assistance for Capt Mills. Task for all workers today 500 baskets. 1400 hrs. Information received that pay could collected later in day. Amt. received at 1900 hrs was Men $1399.30, Medical (2 months) $632.00, Offrs (1 month) $935.00 Balances for Medical (2 months) and Offrs (3 months) will be paid in about ten days time ...

31 July   Working 9 offrs 97 o/rs. Fish issue [illegible] for workers. "Unfit" on 2 meals a day only.

1400 hrs   Coy Comdrs Conference re pay. It was decided to distribute money on following basis:

Lt Col, Maj, Capts	$22.50	Medical certificate holders This accounted for
Lieuts	$15.00	Sgts, S/Sgts $11.00 per month $2464.00 made up
W/Os	$5.00	Cpls $10.00 per month
NCOs	$3.50	L/Cpls $9.00 per month Offrs $555.00 (1 mth)
O/Rs	$3.00 O/Rs	$7.50 per month Med Ords $434 (2 mths)
O/Rs	$1475.00	

Balance of men's pay made up from Offrs & Medical personnel. The remainder $552.30 went into Unit Amenities Fund to be administered by C.O. Full particulars promulgated to men by Paying Officers – also fact that we had no idea of period covered by men's pay.

It was decided that IN FUTURE:

Full Duty personnel in camp receive same rate of pay as workers

Contributions will be required from men to pay sick & to general messing fund to be administrated by C.O.

It is anticipated contributions of Officers & Med personnel will run hospital

Pay will be paid on basis of days worked by men, but some money will be made up to sick men who have done no work.

1 Aug   Good supply of canteen goods obtained unofficially from Harry Lord & co … 500 eggs included – some of them to be gift of English offrs to our hospital patients.

2 Aug   Men employed on railway about 2 kilos from camp. Very wet morning & night. Roads very muddy & slippery. River again in flood – above previous high level. Men had to cross precarious railway bridge on way to & from work. Men NOT knocked off until after dark. Coming home, Sigmn TUZER fell off bridge about 15 feet. Fortunately not seriously injured. Further canteen supplies obtained …

3 Aug   Again very wet. Capt Maruyama annoyed at there being only 3 offrs & 90 o/rs fit for work on railway. He ordered that 200 men be sent out tomorrow. This information conveyed also by I.J.A. guard sgt, Sgt AOKI. He said too that work was now "hurry hurry" as railway would be here in a week (Aug 10). Then we will move to NICKAYE …

4 Aug   Men at work 7 offrs 189 o/rs including about 70 heavy sick. Depressing seeing men moving out … Capt Mills obtained permission from I.J.A. doctor here to send two men – Lieut Dobbie and Pte Rydiard – to English camp 1½ kilos away for operations. Capt MARUYAMA approved. He also approved Capt Barnett taking parties to this camp to collect canteen stores. He also wants same number of men for work tomorrow.

   Last men finished work in the dark at 2145 hrs. They had hazardous journey back to camp along frightfully muddy route. River near "unfit" camp still rising. Offrs had to move their tent. Further canteen supplies obtained from Harry Lord. Two more deaths from cholera today, both 2/29.

5 Aug   6 offrs & 166 men to work (including Camp Duties). Capt MARUYAMA complained of small number & in afternoon asked for 50 more men. Twenty supplied including a party of 12 men who were standing by as a stretcher party. Capt Barnett & Capt Mills saw Capt MARUYAMA at 1515 hrs regarding his authority to move 2 sick men to English camp. Capt Mills also pointed out our position regarding unfit men. Capt Mills then visited English camp to "set up" movement of patients …

6 Aug   Men for work on railway 5 offrs 158 o/rs. Capt Henderson, Lieut May & about [blank] o/rs did NOT get back to camp until midnight – the men having to work till after 2300 hrs. Lieut DOBBIE & Pte RYDIARD carried to English camp in late afternoon. Road wet & slippery … Carriers brought good supply of canteen stores …

7 Aug   Fine – at last. 5 offrs 144 o/rs to work on railway. Capt Barnett reported nos. immediately to Capt MARUYAMA who did NOT show any undue resentment.

Two yaks killed today. Some meat for the troops – at last … 1900 hrs Capt MARUYAMA spoke to Capt Barnett about small no. of officers going to work. Another cholera death – Pte Wallace 2/29 – making 56th death out of original 700.

8 Aug   8 offrs 135 o/rs to work on railway. Heavy sick men still going out. Today, all men were in before it was quite dark, i.e. by 2245 hrs. Two more yaks killed today. Another fine day. 3 men (2/29 & English) to Jap kitchen at camp 3 kilos away.

9 Aug   Fine. 8 offrs 137 o/rs to work. Yak stew & fine weather certainly improves morale of men & offrs. 1900 hrs. Capt Barnett informed by Capt MARUYAMA that all men who did NOT go to work tomorrow would parade at 0900 hrs in railway cutting for inspection …

10 Aug Fine. 8 offrs 135 men to work on railway. At 0930 hrs remainder inspected by Sgt AOKI who picked out only 1 offr … & 10 o/rs from approx. 220 men & sent them out to work. Pte Rydiard died at English camp & was buried in English Cemetery … Two more men (2/29) died here … Some workers did not get back to camp until 2330 hrs …

11 Aug	Fine morning. 8 offrs 114 men to work on railway. Many men not in until 2230 hrs.
1700 hrs	I.J.A. doctor asked Capt Mills to supply names of 150 men who should be evacuated to WYNYEA.

12 Aug　Fine. 6 offrs 98 men only fit for railway work. 1000 hours. Capt MARUYAMA turned out remainder of camp. Personally examined them & sent out a further 9 offrs and 68 o/rs. Most of these men were malaria, diarrhoea, beri-beri, bad feet & ulcers. Some were definitely NOT fit. Task – carrying rice, then working on railway. In view of small number originally going to work, Capt M cancelled killing of yaks today. Therefore no meal.

13 Aug　16 offrs 192 men to work on railway. This included many 'no duties'. Fit and "light duties" working on cutting shifting stone. "No duties" nearer camp moving earth. Both parties out for evening meal despite assurance that latter party would be returning to camp. This party eventually kept at work until 0225 hrs on 14 Aug.

Other party working until nearly 0300 hrs on 14 and back in camp just before 0400 hrs. Capt MARUYAMA told Capt Barnett today men would be working late for next 3 days. When asked by Capt Barnett if they could then have a holiday, (a day's rest), he said his contract finished in 7 days & they could then have a day's rest. Canteen bought 1500 eggs today @ 12 cents. 500 to hospital.

14 Aug　In view of late night only men preparing rock for blasting had to report at 0830 hrs. Remainder at 1000 hrs. All personnel working on rock cutting today. Finished work about 2200 hrs.

No. of personnel for WYNYEA reduced to 70 – the first 70 on list … Probable date of movement 16 AUG. Pte Singer [?] Bde H.Q. died during night 14/15 Aug. following cholera illness.

15 Aug   In view of fact that railway cutting has to be finished today, 200 men were asked for & they had to be on the job at 0830 hrs. Therefore, reveille & breakfast at 0630 hrs. Men supplied on railway 11 offrs 175 o/rs.

Number to be evacuated to WYNYEA tomorrow increased to 80. Four more … died at English Camp, following operation for removal of fluid from lungs, at TAKUNUN.

Men working on railway home at 2345 hrs.

16 Aug
0645 hrs   Party for WYNYEA moved off to river. 0900 hrs. Capt MARUYAMA advised Capt Barnett that 200 fit men – I don't know where the men are coming from – move to hutted camp 2 kilometres north of here. Only personal gear will be taken by men. No tents. Cooking gear will be transported by barge. Only 7 offrs 139 men fit for railway work. Capt M insisted on another 30 who had to go out. Promised light work but working on railway with other party … Personnel remaining at TAKUNUN now 17 offrs 380 men … 2300 hrs. Capt M advised party would not move tomorrow – possibly 18 AUG. Men on railway working until nearly 0300 hrs. Condensed milk issue for 3rd successive night. One small tin between 2 men.

17 Aug   Reveille for rock drillers as usual. Others 0945 hrs & to report to I.J.A. camp at 1100 hrs. … Men working until 2230 hrs and home by 2330 hrs.
2345 hrs   Advice received that moving party to be reduced to one hundred. Remainder to complete cutting here then to move. Task in new locality (2 kilometres from here) will take about 1 week. Then men return.

18 Aug
0900 hrs   4 offrs 72 o/rs reported for work here on railway. Other party of 4 offrs … 7 cooks and 85 o/rs moved to new site. Accommodation – attap huts. Cooking gear transported

by river. Only personal gear carried. 14 light duty men to clean huts – others to work on railway immediately. Cpl Johnston (2/29 Btn) died after prolonged illness.

2100 hrs   Pay received. Officers $2305.00 (3 mths …). Medical orderlies $252.00 (adjustment made in respect of 9 men who have NOT got their original Red Cross certificates and who therefore the I.J.A. will NOT recognise as entitled to special allowance), o/rs $417.90 – representing pay due for period 21 JUL – 31 JUL 43 (incl.) It was mentioned, too, that the $1395.30 received on 30 JUL was in respect of period 21 JUN – 20 JUL 43. The reason given that men had received no money for period 18 APR – 20 JUN was that "some men had run away. Therefore no money". Men worked until 2100 hrs today.

19 Aug   Wet. 4 more men reported to Capt Lloyd's party. Working here on railway 3 offrs 54 o/rs. Men worked until 2100 hrs today. Rain spoilt easy day.

20 Aug   3 offrs 73 men to work on railway. Capt M & Japs helping remove landslide in cutting "speedo". Men paid …

Men back in camp by 2200 hrs today. Rumours still current that we shall return to Changi when railway is through. 15 original "carriers" in cholera isolation returned to No Duty area.

21 Aug   For work on railway 3 offrs 66 o/rs. Additional 40 men required by Capt M. Sgt AOKI paraded remaining men in camp and picked out 27 who were sent out to work. For the first time some consideration was given to no [illegible] & men with bad feet. Today Capt M. pulled them off parade & sent them on a sit down job helping rock blasters. Lt Col Pond & Capt Mills visited other camp – 1100 hrs to 2000 hrs. Work conditions good but track to place of work very bad. Rations – rice (about 30 ozs per day per man), fish, meat, vegetables, sugar & tea.

22 Aug	Party here still on cutting (3 offrs 77 o/rs). Capt Barnett visited other camp. Bamboo shoots are popular part of their diet. Capt MARUYAMA informed Capt Barnett this morning it was improbable any more men would move to other camp.
2130 hrs	Information received that it was necessary to send evening meal out to working party as the men would be working until 0300 hrs. "Muchen" (makan = meal?) went out, men worked for 10 minutes after meal, then returned to camp, arriving at 0035 hrs. They received "presents' of hot coffee, condensed milk (as usual, one small tin between two) …
23 Aug	Working here 3 offrs 88 o/rs. Additional party of 30 men called for in afternoon to carry rations from barge to Jap store. Information says these stores are milk & cigarettes – to be "presents" to Australians from Japanese Government. Workers home about 2230 hrs.
24 Aug	Fine morning. 3 offrs 80 o/rs to work. Fall of earth in cutting buried Lieut Lilly, half buried [two privates] … None seriously injured. Japs worked feverishly to free men. Men working until about 2400 hrs. Soup issue (from English camp … through Capt Barnett) to 99 men at other camp …
25 Aug	Fine morning. 2 offrs 78 o/rs to work. Capt Barnett spoke to Capt MARUYAMA regarding towgay (bean sprouts) & increase in meat ration. Both received today. Capt M. proceeding NICKAYE today. We shall be moved in 8 or 10 days back to TAIMONTA probably – Capt M. will look out good camp site during his trip. Only fit men will move carrying personal gear. Sick men will remain here until transported to BANPONG. Our tents, working gear to be transported by barge.
0845 hrs	Both Capt MARUYAMA & Sgt AOKI approved of Sgt MENTILOW's [?] transfer to English Hospital. Men worked until 2400 hrs. Rain & wind about 2300 hrs blew

several tents to ribbons. Railway reached cutting about 2 kilos south of TARKANUN.

26 Aug   2 offrs 26 o/rs to work on railway. Sgt AOKI brought 3 offrs & 31 o/rs down by barge from TARARUMPET …

2300 hrs   Sigmn KIRK fell off railway bridge. Dropped about 25 feet & fairly seriously injured.

27 Aug   2 offrs 74 o/rs to work on railway … Unfit personnel for evacuation down the river inspected by Japanese doctor. 80 selected. Cholera tested (glass rod) in afternoon …

28 Aug   Kirk's injury bad dislocation of hip. Rectified by Major Pemberton [C.O. English Base Hospital Group 2].

1600 hrs   Sgt Mentilow [?] died at English Hospital. Information received to the effect that all fit men will move back to TAIMONTA probably on 3/9/43.

29 Aug
0800 hrs   Surprise kit inspection by I.J.A. Very thorough.
1700 hrs   WYNYEA party standing by ready to move.

30 Aug
1200 hrs   Sigmn Kirk brought back from English Hospital. He replaces Sigmn Mullens in WYNYEA draft. Men worked until 2330 hrs tonight.

31 Aug
0545 hrs   Reveille for WYNYEA party.
0700 hrs   Party moved to barge …

1 Sep
0830 hrs   Capt Barnett saw Capt MARUYAMA regarding move. Sick & light duties will move first (3 or 4 Sep) and may take 4-6 days. Additional rice required would have to be carried. Fit will move on 5 Sep. Food will be provided at staging camps. Permission was granted for some canteen

supplies to be transported by barge with cooking gear and tents. Request was made for Lt. Col Pond to travel by barge (O.K.'d later). All torn tents to be taken down & returned Japanese lines.

2 offrs 66 o/rs to work on railway. Home by 2130 hrs. Quiet day – fine. 2000 hrs. Information received from Korean guard that 60 men could remain here – 30 heavy sick, 12 cholera, 14 light sick, 2 cooks, 2 medical orderlies & they would move to KONKOIDA (when) recovered.

2 Sep	Fine. A Holiday. Reveille 0745 hrs. Further information received that 60 men remain here, 100 men move on 3 SEP (these will be light sick) & remaining 66 move on 5 SEP. Lt. Col. Pond & 3 o/rs will travel with gear on barge. Men's blankets will also be carried if required.
1830 hrs	Lt. Col. Pond, Capt Mills & Capt Barnett dined with Capt Lord at English camp.
2000 hrs	Tenko.
3 Sep	Dull but no rain.
0900 hrs	6 offrs 94 o/rs moved off under Capt Curlewis. Movement to be very slow. 2 lbs rice & 2 fish carried as reserve rations. 1 offr 31 o/rs to work on railway. Half holiday at camp 2 kilos away.
4 Sep	No work on railway. Packing etc in preparation for move tomorrow. Afternoon transport of goods to barges. 3 cases of milk, 6 tins gula Malacca, 24 tins of biscuits taken as canteen stores.
5 Sep	
0600 hrs	Reveille. Tents struck & taken with personal gear to barge. Lt. Col. Pond and 2 o/rs travelling by barge. 0800 hrs. 3 offrs (Capts Werdersehn (?), Barnett & Graham) and 61 o/rs left by road for TAIMONTA … Marching party made TAMARUMPET by 1700 hrs & here spent the night. Early part of track fair (only railway route) last

2 kilos very bad. Our party were housed in attap hut, Capt Hardacre's party, which had left their camp about 0900 hrs, were camped in tents – filthy & inadequate for their 99 men.

6 Sep   Moved off from TAMARUMPET at 0900 hrs … Made KRIEN KRIE about 1730 hrs (14 kilos). Track very bad – wet & muddy. Billeted by people of D Force. "Weather" good.

7 Sep   Moved off from KRIEN KRIE at 0900 hrs. Made KONKOIDA (9 kilos) for lunch. Then TAIMONTA (further 12 kilos) for night. Camped in attap hut, shared by [illegible]. Track during the day for the most part shocking, particularly from KONKOIDA onwards. Caught up here with Capt Curlewis's party. Total party now 14 offrs 272 o/rs.

8 Sep
0745 hrs   Reveille.
0750 hrs   Tenko. Men worked on clearing area for new camp site., gathering bamboo & carrying goods from barge (river approx. 1½ kilos away) … Wet afternoon.

9 Sep   72 o/rs carrying stores etc from river. 76 o/rs clearing site for new camp & carrying bamboo.
1400 hrs   Further cholera test (glass rod), malaria blood test & cholera inoculation. Men finished work by 2030 hrs.

10 Sep   3 parties today – 20 o/rs carrying stores from river, 20 o/rs clearing, 112 o/rs bamboo carrying & hut building … Men in from work by 2030 hrs.

11 Sep   Wet morning. Work parties 1 offr 20 o/rs bamboo, 2 offrs 133 o/rs railway. OKAMURA collected reserve ration of rice from personnel remaining in camp.
0900 hrs   A/CSM Cunningham left for NICKAYE on canteen buying expedition.

12 Sep   165 men requested by me could only supply 153. Malaria & foot sores & ulcers main illnesses. It looks as if we shall be moving from this double-decker attap hut (which we are sharing with Tamils) to our new camp in about 4 or 5 days. Work on railway etc. NOT arduous.

13 Sep   Cunningham returned from NICKAYE … Canteen supplies dearer than at TAKUNUN and goodly quantity bought. He also brought back gift from I.J.A. – 186 pairs of white shorts, 2179 packets of cigarettes (10 per pkt), 40 tins condensed milk, and 3 tins of margarine. Cigarettes distributed at rate of 7 packets per man. Pay cheque for officers & medical signed today.

14 Sep   4 offrs 151 men to work on railway. Party of 20 (4 offrs, C.S.M. etc) started draining new camp area. Very wet in afternoon. Latter party sent home then recalled by Capt M. Design of huts altered from island platform (?) to that of aisle down centre. All men in from work by 2015 hrs.

15 Sep   155 to work on railway. 15 offrs & men to new camp area. Bearers of 3 huts erected by Burmese …

16 Sep
0900 hrs   Working parties as usual. Capt Barnett to NIEKE to collect pay. Track wet & muddy. Railway between TAIMONTA & NIEKE defined & cut in sections. Many "boongs" at work tunnelling [?]. Still a lot of work to be done.
1500 hrs   Lt. Col. Kappe arrived at NIEKE from No.1 Camp [21 kilos north]. He has received a note from Major Jacobs [A Force]. This force has been well treated.

17 Sep   Working parties as usual.

18 Sep   Capt MARUYAMA inspected sick with view to increasing work figure … Capt Barnett received pay as follows:

Officers $850.00 (August) Capt & above $50.00 (9) Lieuts $40.00 (10)

Med Ords $189.00 (August) Sgts $20.00, Cpls $20.00, L/cpls $10 O/rs $9

O/rs Period 11/5/43 to 20/6/43 $3,021.15

Period 1/8/43 to 31/8/43 $1,659.80

Period 1/9/43 to 10/9/43 $425.70 Grand Total $6,143.65

Party on railway working until midnight in rain.

19 Sep   Very wet. Working parties 127 & camp construction 12. Pay to all ranks.

20 Sep   170 men asked for for railway. Could only supply 145. Wet day. All men in from work by 2030 hrs. 3 offrs 4 o/rs working on new campsite in afternoon.

2100 hrs   Information received that party would be moving to new campsite tomorrow morning immediately after breakfast.

21 Sep
0830 hrs   Party moved to new area. Huts roofed but no sides. Approx. 100 in each of 3 huts. As only about 120 fit for work, MORIYAMA (guard) paraded sick & sent out additional 30 … Wet afternoon.

22 Sep
0750 hrs   TENKO 160 men sent to work including 30 heavy sick. C.S.M. Cunningham and Lieut Gillies to NIEKE with Sgt AOKI to purchase canteen supplies. Covering for cook-house completed – the first decent covering (attap) since leaving Changi.

23 Sep   During night 22/23 about $30.00 stolen from canteen. No work but working party fell in at 0830 hrs. Some delay whilst Japs endeavoured to make total from 155 (including approx. 40 heavy sick) to 160. Wet afternoon …

24 Sep   140 men to work. 4 hospital orderlies & some other heavy sick pulled out to make up party.

1300 hrs   Lieut Gillies & C.S.M. Cunningham returned from NIEKE with $2,300.00 worth canteen supplies. Portion of goods carried from river during afternoon.

25 Sep   141 men to work. Balance of canteen supplies transported from river. All commodities were rationed to enable every man to obtain an equal share.

Moriyama had meeting of C.S.M.s about 2030 hrs and told them we had to supply 170 tomorrow. Capt Barnett saw Moriyama who was adamant (he stated that all medical orderlies except 3 and all officers except C.O., Adjt, Padre & M.O. must work), so Capt Barnett then saw Capt MARUYAMA. He said the same number as today would suffice and allowed us to retain medical orderlies, but he said that work must repeat must be completed in 4 days – implying that this must be done even if men had to work late at night. He also instructed that 2 men be sent to TONKOIDA tomorrow to bring back 15 yaks. Lids must also be made for latrines & drinking water must be passed through the filter. Men must be quieter at night & in early morning. Lights out, therefore, made 2300 hrs – same as I.J.A.

Yaks which were stuck in the mud near Capt Hardacre's working party, killed. I.J.A. & Burmese took most of the meat … party of 40 men working until 0030 hrs on 26/9.

First completely fine day for some time.

26 Sep   150 men to work.

0900 hrs   Two men left for KONKOIDA to bring back yaks. Returned at 2000 hrs with 15 beasts. Another fine day …

Hot wash available to workers [2 Coys a fortnight] on arrival home. Two parties working until 2300 hrs.

2200 hrs   Capt M. informed Capt Barnett (i) all I.J.A. officers must be saluted by ALL ranks – if working, only i/c party salutes (ii) no noise between lights out (2300 hrs) & reveille (0730 hrs).

27 Sep   140 men to work. Another fine day. Sgt AOKI arrived back from NIEKE & stated definitely we shall be returning to CHANGI as soon as railway is finished. Last two of three working parties in by 2200 hrs. …

28 Sep   132 men to work today. Still fine. 1500 hrs. … One yak killed today – we receive frame only for 292 men. Men in from work by 2200 hrs. "Back to Changi" very definite, according to our guards, about middle of October.

29 Sep   125 men to work. Capt MILLS beaten up by Sgt AOKI. Weather fine. I.J.A. started to dig slit trenches.

30 Sep   156 men to work. Improvement due to fine weather and yak. Some canteen supplies (3 tins gula malacca - palm sugar) obtained from local kampong. Guards generous – eggs [illegible] from HARADA. All workers in by 2130 hrs.

1 Oct   142 all ranks to work today … Two parties working until 0230 hrs on 2/10 – a wet night too. Sweet coffee put on from amenities for all workers.

2 Oct   130 all ranks to work. …
Fine day. Sweet coffee for all men. Capt (Graham?) & 26 o/rs (sick men) working until 0200 hrs on 3/10/43.

3 Oct   130 all ranks to work. Fine day. All men in by 2100 hrs. Rumours that work will be completed in 2 days.

4 Oct   134 all ranks to work … Fine day. Work finished 2030 hrs. Rumours are now we move to KAMBURIE & stay there for a period before moving back to CHANGI and – Railway work for our lads finished in 3 days.

5 Oct   131 all ranks to work. Another fine & hot day following cold night. Men in by 2030 hrs.

6 Oct   130 men to work. 0850 Capt Barnett left for NIEKE to collect pay for period 11-30 SEP.

7 Oct   Information received that all personnel of our party now at NIEKE and beyond had been paid at their respective camps for period 11 MAY – 20 JUNE 43.

8 Oct   130 men to work.
1915 hrs   Capt Barnett returned from NIEKE. Men finished approach to bridge and all in by 2030 hrs.

9 Oct
0830 hrs   Glass rod & blood slide for all men. 0900 hrs. 138 men to work with promise that only fit men – about 100 – would be required from tomorrow onwards. Pay day for all ranks. Amounts received from NIEKE were as follows:- Officers $850.00, Medical Orderlies $177 plus $21.00 in respect of orderlies without Red Cross Certificates (1 Cpl, 1 L/Cpl, 2 Ptes at heavy work rate), O/rs $846.10 (excluding $21.00 in respect of Med Orderlies) …

All men finished work at 2000 hrs. Work NOT arduous. Return submitted of all men with serviceable boots (18) shirts (75) and shorts (60).

10 Oct   113 all ranks to work on railway. NO "hurry hurry".
As all men beyond NIEKE had been paid for period May-June, it was decided to grant a bonus of $0.50 to all men (excl. Med Orderlies) at TAIMONTA (257), TARKUNUN (46) and WYNYEA (206). 1800 hrs Capt Barnett saw Capt M. re meat for men & improvement in rations. Would NOT say whether or not yak was to be killed nor would he give us permission to buy a yak from our own funds. He said we would have to supply 200 men & was told that was impossible. He also said all fit officers would have to work.

11 Oct   164 all ranks (7 offrs) to work. Other sick personnel cleaning up around camp, about one hour morning & afternoon. Railway work finished 2000 hrs.

12 Oct   149 all ranks (7 offrs) to work. 1000-1100 sick grass cutting.
1500-1700 hrs   Same. Railway personnel widening cutting adjacent to camp. In by 2030 hrs. Food still rice (or gruel) & weak stew of fish & potatoes.

13 Oct   127 all ranks (5 offrs) to work on cutting … Sick (4 offrs 35 o/rs) grass cutting as usual.
1930 hrs   2,240 packets of cigarettes (10) and a large supply of toilet paper received. Cigarettes distributed 6½ packets per man (including 52 TARKUNUN personnel). Nips evidently had an issue of whisky today &, with Capt M. away, they celebrated.

14 Oct   153 all ranks (6 offrs) to work. 0835 Report received that Pte (Ambie?) & Crawford had NOT slept in their beds. Sgt AOKI organised search & men were found tied to posts at coolie camp 400 yds away. They went there last night to change Burmese rupees for Thai dollars & were "bashed up". "Presents" cigarettes withdrawn from all men in camp. Information is these will later be distributed to "[illegible] men". Men working until 2030 hrs.

15 Oct   144 all ranks (6 offrs) to work. Railway lines passed our camp at 1015 hrs …1 offr 43 men of our party breaking stones for ballast today … Sigmn Hunter caught by NIPS taking sweet potatoes outside Q.M. store. Done over. Workers home by 2030 hrs.

16 Oct   148 all ranks (6 offrs) to work … Men finished work at 1930 hrs.

17 Oct   130 all ranks (6 offrs) to work. Most prevalent illnesses malaria (mostly recurring) and diarrhoea …

1800 hrs	Church Service in hospital.
2130 hrs	Concert being given to hospital patients stopped by Capt MARUYAMA. Five singers "beaten up" and orders received that there must be no music or singing in Unit lines. (On two occasions recently our guards have come over at night and asked Capt Barnett to get Australians to sing).
18 Oct	138 all ranks (6 offrs) to work.
0845	Order re music & singing passed on to troops. Men in by 1930 hrs. No canteen supplies could be purchased today and, as a result, amenities could not supply guala malacca for breakfast as it has been doing for about last 10 days. Sweet coffee at night can be continued for another 6 nights. Food is still bad – rice & weak stew.
19 Oct	135 all ranks (6 offrs) to work. 100 men & 4 offrs to NIEKE – per boat – to collect picks, shunkels [?] etc. Lunch had to be carried to meet them returning … Party arrived back carrying: anvils, box of tools in addition to shovels, axes etc. Carried vegetables on way to NIEKE from UPPER TAIMONTA. Rumours now that this party shall soon be moving to NIEKE as KAMBURIE is overcrowded.
20 Oct	135 all ranks (6 offrs) to work. Another party of 100 men & 4 offrs to NIEKE. Lt. Col. Pond NOT permitted to make trip with party. Lunch carried on man. Party home by 1830 hrs having carried back boxes. Excellent lunch provided at NIEKE by Dutchmen. Canteen supplies very scarce here.
21 Oct	138 all ranks (6 offrs) to work. More than enough volunteers for NIEKE party. Carried back boxes & home by 1900 hrs. Yak killed today – first for about 20 days. Weather – cool nights, hot afternoons. Sgt AOKI ordered all men in camp to make fly swats & kill 10 flies per day.

22 Oct   NIEKE party reduced to 2 offrs & 48 o/rs. Balance at work on railway 4 offrs 68 o/rs. NIEKE party loaded goods on train, travelled to UPPER KONKOIDA. Unloaded, walked back. Home by 1800 hrs.

23 Oct   127 (6 offrs) to work. 1 offr 25 o/rs grass cutting. Weather still good. Yak killed today.

24 Oct   120 (6 offrs) to work. Party of 2 offrs 48 o/rs to KONKOIDA carrying gear. 1 offr 20 o/rs grass cutting. KONKOIDA party carried down picks, shovels etc.. Brought back milk, biscuits, peanut [?] coffee for I. J. A.. YASTA went to TAMARUMPAT to purchase canteen stores for us.

25 Oct   Holiday. Ceremony of linking up railway near KONKOIDA.

1130 hrs   "Presents" 1344 pckts of cigarettes. Distribution 4½ packets per man. "Presents" of [illegible] & peanut [?] coffee to offrs from Sgt AOKI & HARADA.

26 Oct   129 (6 offrs) to work. Two parties. Easy day.

27 Oct   (6 offrs) to work. Two parties.

0600   YASTA arrived back from TAMARUMPET with canteen supplies 54 tins of biscuits, 2 bags of sugar, 96 tins milk, 96 tins fish (prices resp. $3.75 per tin, $165.00 per bag, $2.75 per tin, $2.75 per tin). Allotment made to hospital, coys (companies) & officers. One bag of sugar purchased from amenities to provide sweet gruel for men in morning & sweet coffee at night. [Illegible] beaten up by Sgt AOKI for losing 2 yaks. Some rain today.

28 Oct   127 (6 offrs) to work. Two parties. One of 109 (6 offrs) took lunch – carrying party to KONKOIDA, picks, axes, boxes etc.. Other party working in quarry. Fine day.

29 Oct (6 offrs) to work. Carrying party to KONKOIDA. Small party in quarry.

0855 hrs Capt Barnett to NIEKE for pay. Pay received $797.15, overtime $96.55. Total $893.70. Information received that TARKANOON party move to KAMBURIE tomorrow. Nominal roll of all our personnel as at 1 NOV 43 required at NIEKE not later than 5 NOV 43. …

30 Oct 123 (6 offrs) to work. Carrying party for KONKOIDA. Small party in quarry. Pay Day. C.O. approved of bonus of $0.25 for all men at TAIMONTA to be paid out of overtime. Coy claims (incl bonus) were as follows

1 Coy (77)	$244.35	
2 Coy (64)	$186.50	
3 Coy (54)	$163.00	
4 Coy (63)	$203.50	
TARKANOON	$66.40	
Balance to amenities	$29.95	$893.70

Rumours that the party will be moving to NIEKE in 6 days time

31 Oct No further road work. All walking personnel at KONKOIDA (116) or NIEKE (4). Movement by train men paraded at 0830 hrs and after waiting an hour were sent back to huts to wait arrival of train.

1030 hrs "Presents" of approx. 4,450 pckts of cigarettes (15 pckts per man) and 13 tins of margarine. Party did NOT go to KONKOIDA – only loaded train here with Nips gear.

1700 hrs Capt MARUYAMA and [illegible] Nip soldiers left for KONKOIDA. We are now left with our guards & 12 Nips.

Index